the
creative jeweler

the creative jeweler

inspirational projects using semi-precious and everyday materials

Sharon McSwiney, Penny Williams,
Claire C Davies, Jennie Davies

krause publications

700 EAST STATE ST., IOLA, WI 54990-0001
(715) 445-2214
www.krause.com

A QUINTET BOOK

Please call or write for our free catalog of publications. Our toll-free number to
place an order or obtain a free catalog is 800-258-0929 or please use our regular
business telephone 715-445-2214 for editorial comment and further information.

Library of Congress Catalog Number 99–67513
ISBN 0-87341-556-6

This book was designed and produced by
Quintet Publishing Limited
The Old Brewery
6 Blundell Street
London N7 9BH, UK

Creative Editor: Richard Dewing
Art Director: Paula Marchant
Designer: Jacqui Ellis Dodd
Project Editor: Laura Price
Photography: Paul Forrester

Typeset in Great Britain by
Central Southern Typesetters, Eastbourne
Manufactured in China by Regent Publishing Services Ltd.
Printed in Singapore by Star Standard Pte. Ltd.

Contents

Introduction

Jewelry is often considered to be an expensive accessory. This book sets out to explain in simple steps how to produce stylish and modern necklaces, bracelets, brooches, and earrings that are individual and expressive in design, while also developing basic skills in the art of jewelry making. A wealth of inspirational ideas backs up each of the projects and offers the reader an ideal introduction to the creation of modern pieces.

All of the projects are laid out in easy to follow steps, illustrated with helpful demonstration photographs. A wide spectrum of processes use materials ranging from precious metals to everyday "found" objects and recycled paper, and techniques such as beadwork, wirework, and metal forming are used to create exciting and innovative designs. The projects also vary in complexity, so that the maker can develop confidence while mastering a variety of skills from the straightforward to the complex.

This project-based book is intended to inspire and illustrate that jewelry does not necessarily have to be made from precious metal and gemstones, or require lots of specialist equipment. Indeed, the dictionary definition of jewelry reads, "Any item worn or used for adornment." Jewelry can be made from a whole host of materials.

It can be fun or even ephemeral. In the past, earrings, brooches, and necklaces have been created from hair, bone, coal, or glass. In some non-Western cultures, natural resources such as seeds, feathers, clay, bird and animal skulls, and bones are used.

Recycling is a key element in some of the projects in this book. Throughout history, old or unfashionable jewelry has been broken up and remade in the current style. Modern recycling has included the use of aluminum cans, telephone wire, and bottle tops in the creation of new jewelery design.

As well as new and recycled material, jewelry can be made from "found" objects. These could be items which evoke memories of past events, or things collected from nature which inspire jewelery design.

Some techniques in jewelry making do require highly specialist and expensive equipment; however, with such basics as a piercing saw frame, snips, and some pliers, plus the help of the projects set out in this book, it is possible to create pieces of jewelry which are both innovatively designed and very professional in appearance, and which can be altered to be worn on any occasion.

Materials

Sheet Metal

The metals most commonly used in jewelry making can be split into two main groups: non-ferrous such as copper, brass, tin, and aluminum, or precious such as silver and gold.

Copper – Pinkish red in color, malleable, and easy to work with, it is readily available in both sheet and wire form.

Brass – Pale yellow in color and a harder metal than copper.

Sterling silver – Softer than either copper or brass, containing 925 parts in 1000 of fine silver. It is available from specialist refiners or bullion dealers, most of whom will allow you to purchase small quantities at a time. You can often select from off-cuts or pieces can be cut to a specific size.

Findings

This is the term applied to the small components used in jewelry making, such as earring clips, stems, or posts, and backs. These can be bought ready-made from specialist suppliers or craft stores and are available in precious and plated base metal forms.

Jump rings are the small rings of wire which are often used to link components together and attach earring hooks.

Modeling Plastic

Available in strips and blocks, it comes in various colors and finishes and is obtainable from art and craft stores.

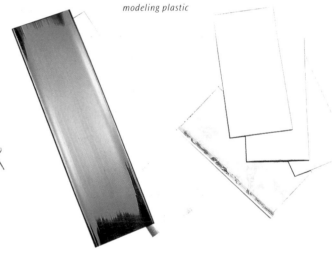

modeling plastic

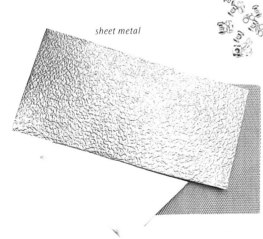

sheet metal

earring stems, posts, and backs

jump rings

glitter pens

Glitter Pens

Pens containing ready-mixed glue and glitter which are available from good stationery stores. Always read the instructions to ensure that you cause no damage to fabrics and plastics. These can be used as an alternative to paints for those projects where paint is used to decorate jewelry.

Beads and Sequins

Thousands of bead variations from different countries in innumerable sizes, shapes, and colors are available. They are most often made from ceramics, glass, plastic, metal, or wood. Most craft stores will stock beads of some description and there are shops specializing only in beads.

Oven-Bake Clay

A plastic modeling material which is baked in the oven to harden. It is sold in small blocks and there are numerous colors available. This clay is available in most art and craft stores.

oven-bake clay

self-hardening clay

Self-Hardening Clay

This clay substance hardens on contact with air and therefore requires no baking or firing. It is available in terracotta or white and can be obtained from art and craft stores.

beads and sequins

Paints and Inks

Enamel paint – Many different colors are produced in both matte and transparent varieties. Available in small pots from hardware, model, or craft stores, enamel paint requires 4 to 6 hours of drying time. Clean the brushes you have used with enamel thinners.

enamel paint

Inks – Colored water-based inks used for coloring and staining surfaces can be bought in small pots from art or stationery stores and come in a wide variety of colors, including gold and silver. Ink can be used as a wood stain or an alternative to paint.

inks

Other Paints

These can be used to decorate paper and card-based projects instead of the more metalic enamel paints.

Gouache paint – A good quality poster paint that is sold in art stores. Available in tubes or pots in a wide spectrum of colors, it is water-soluble and dries quickly.

Acrylic paint – Obtainable from art stores, in pot or tube form, in a wide variety of colors.

gouache paint

acrylic paint

thick silk ribbon

rubber tube

Leather Thong

Leather thong is available in a range of thicknesses and colors. It is flexible, durable, and strong, which makes it easy to knot and to thread quantities of beads without fear of the thong breaking.

Thick Silk Ribbon

Thick silk ribbon is available in a variety of widths, colors, and textures. It is excellent to use in the creation of close-fitting chokers.

Rubber Tube

Rubber tube can be found in most auto supply stores. It is easy to cut and makes simple yet effective parts for jewelry.

Thick Linen Thread

Thick linen thread is available in a range of neutral colors which complement natural beads. It is easy to knot and so creates a good base structure for threading beads. It can be purchased waxed and unwaxed. The wax provides a protective coating which makes the thread more durable and it creates a sheen on the surface of the thread, which adds to the effect of the jewelery.

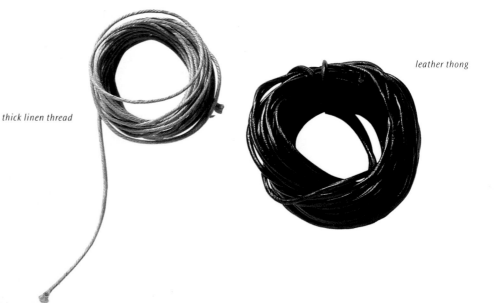

thick linen thread

leather thong

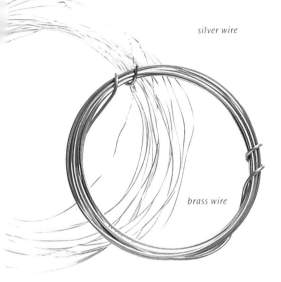

silver wire

brass wire

copper wire

Silver, Brass, and Copper Wire

Metal wire is available in a variety of thicknesses. It is usually sold in a softened or annealed state so that it is easy to manipulate. The most widely used type of wire is round in section. This and various other shapes, such as half-round, square, oval, and rectangular in section, are available from most good art and model making stores.

Newspaper

Utilize the versatility of paper and recycle old newspapers to create durable, wearable, individual necklaces.

Cabochon and Faceted Glass Stones

These stones are flat-backed and foiled to create highly reflective surfaces which give a jewel-like quality and can be easily set into a self-hardening modeling clay.

cabochon and faceted glass stones

newspaper

Tools and Equipment

Wire Wool
Used for cleaning the surface of sheet metal, it removes grease and dirt, leaving a satin finish.

Pliers
There are many different shapes of pliers, the most commonly used being (see below, from left to right), half round, round-nosed, and flat-nosed. They are used for shaping, curling, bending, and flattening wire.

Center Punch
The center punch is a rod of steel with a point on the end and is used to make an indentation in metal before drilling a hole. Sometimes it is used to punch a texture.

Tin Snips
Snips or shears come in a variety of sizes and are used for cutting flat sheet metal in straight lines or simple curves.

wire wool

tin snips

pliers

center punch

Wooden Jeweler's Peg and G Clamp

The clamp is used to secure the jeweler's peg to a sturdy table top. The wooden peg is then used as a support for metal which is being cut, shaped, and filed.

Jeweler's Piercing Saw

This saw is used for cutting all types of sheet metal. Different size blades are available for cutting different thicknesses of metal.

Wire Cutters

They come in a variety of sizes depending on the thickness of wire to be cut. Occasionally wire cutters are incorporated within a pair of pliers.

Hammers

Chasing Hammer – With a polished flat surface on one end and a ball shape on the other, this hammer is useful for flattening or texturing metal.

Ball Pein Hammer – Less expensive than the chasing hammer, but used in the same way.

Nylon Mallet – Useful for flattening metal without marking the surface.

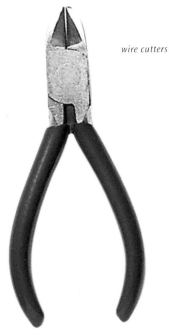

wire cutters

wooden jeweler's peg and G clamp

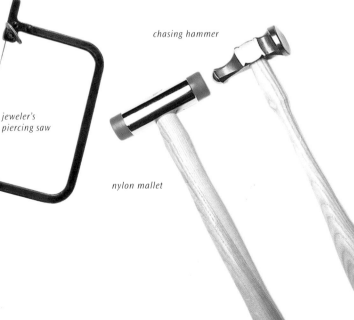

chasing hammer

jeweler's piercing saw

nylon mallet

metal scriber

drill

files

Metal Scriber

A hardened steel rod, tapered to a sharp point, used to score lines into metal surfaces. These lines can be functional, such as one to follow when cutting, or simply decorative.

Drill

A tool for making holes of various sizes in different materials. Special jeweler's hand drills are available, but a small general purpose drill from hardware stores will be perfectly adequate, provided the chuck will hold small size drill bits. Useful sizes of drill bits to obtain are $\frac{1}{32}$ inch and $\frac{3}{32}$ inch.

Files

Files are used to remove unwanted burrs or blemishes on the edges of metal surfaces, to enlarge holes, or bevel edges. Various types are available, with small needle files being particularly useful. There are also different shapes and cuts, 00 being the coarsest and 6 the finest. The teeth on a file only cut on the forward stroke, therefore the file should be lifted on the backward stroke so that it is not in contact with the metal.

Adhesives

Resin-based glue (epoxy) – A strong bonding glue which requires the mixing of an adhesive and hardener to enable it to work, it is available in tube form or in a syringe. Follow manufacturers' instructions carefully.

All Purpose Clear, Strong Adhesive – Useful for sticking non-metal items such as wood, fabric, and some plastics together, it is available in tubes. Use in a well-ventilated area.

PVA – A white non-toxic, water-based glue, it is particularly suitable for bonding paper, card, and fabrics. Available in tubes or plastic bottles, it can be applied with a brush. Rinse the brush under water immediately after use.

resin-based glue

all purpose clear, strong adhesive

pva

Techniques

Hammering

The basic techniques used in the projects are explained here, most of which are various methods of making fasteners or findings for necklaces. Ready-made fasteners can be bought from most jewelry suppliers but, because the findings are quite simple, by making them yourself they can become an integral part of the necklace rather than something that is added on at the end.

Metal Texture can be created by hammering a metal surface. Hold the hammer handle with a firm grip toward the end, with the index finger extended along the handle for support. Do not "batter" the metal but apply rhythmic taps.

Nylon Mallet Hammering with a nylon mallet flattens sheet metal or wire without having an effect on the surface.

Wire Wire can be flattened and textured by hammering. The wire will also be hardened and will therefore keep its form better.

Center Punch A center punch can be used to create decorative punched dots on a metal surface. Hold the punch vertically to the metal and lightly tap the top with a flat-sided hammer.

center-punched and saw-pierced metal

Drilling

1 Before drilling a metal surface it is important to center-punch the place where you want the hole to be. This will prevent the drill from skating over the surface and give it a precise starting point.

2 Hold the drill in a vertical position. Start to turn the handle slowly to enable the drill bit to bite, but do not put any pressure on the drill or the drill bit may break.

The piercing saw is used to cut the center for the Enameled Brooch (see page 76)

Sawing Metal

1 Use a piercing saw frame and a blade. Blades come in a variety of sizes depending on the metal you need to cut. Make sure the blade has the rough side pointing out from the frame and the teeth pointing down toward the ground. Open the nut and bolt at the top of the frame. Trap the blade in the gap provided and screw it back together as tightly as possible.

2 Prop the saw frame into the peg. Lower the other end of the blade between the other nut and bolt. Push your weight against the frame while tightening the blade in position. Release the weight and the blade should be held in position under tension. If there is any movement in the blade, it is not tight enough.

3 Hold the metal firmly over the peg. Keeping the saw at a 90-degree angle to the ground, gently move it forward. The saw will only cut on the down stroke. Do not push too hard because the thin blades break very easily. Take your time to master using the saw.

Sawing a Hole or Pattern in the Center of a Piece of Metal

1 Make a center-punch mark on the metal at the edge of the shape you need to cut.

2 Drill a small hole through the center punch mark, large enough for the piercing blade to fit through.

Ornate shapes such as this are best cut using a piercing saw.

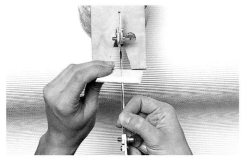

3 Open one end of the piercing saw and thread the blade through the hole. Tighten up the blade again.

4 Hold the metal firmly against the peg and cut out the desired shape.

Completed bead wires (see page 121)

Bead Wires

1 Cut a length of wire approximately 1 inch longer in length than the beads to be threaded.

2 Secure one end of the wire in a pair of round-nosed pliers and carefully bend the wire to create a loop.

3 Thread the beads onto the wire, pushing them up to the looped end of the wire.

4 With the round-nosed pliers, make another loop in the other end of the wire to secure the beads.

Jump Rings

1 Cut a 6-inch length of wire, secure one end in a pair of round-nosed pliers, and slowly bend the wire around one side of the pliers to create the beginning of a coil.

2 Continue to coil the wire around the pliers until all of the wire is used and a regular coil of wire is formed.

3 Remove the coil from the pliers and, using a pair of wire snips, cut up one side of the coil.

  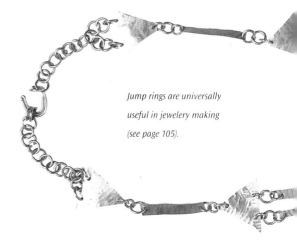

4 The jump rings can be opened using two pairs of flat-nosed pliers; another jump ring can then be threaded on, and the host jump ring closed.

5 A chain can be created from the jump rings by repeating the process of linking jump rings, one after another.

Jump rings are universally useful in jewelery making (see page 105).

Twisting Wire

1 With wire snips, cut two equal 48-inch lengths of wire and bend them both in half. Secure the ends in a vise. Take a hooked piece of wire, which is fastened into a drill, and hook it onto the looped end of the bent wires.

2 Turn the hand drill to make the wires twist together. It is important to turn the drill slowly to allow the wires to twist together evenly.

3 Continue to turn the drill until the wires are tightly and evenly twisted together along the length of the wire. You can choose how loosely or tightly twisted you want your wire to be.

4 Remove the twisted wires from the vise and drill. Using the wire snips, cut off the looped end, so you are left with an even length of wire.

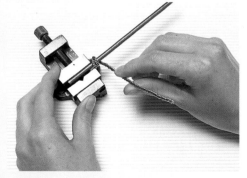

5 Secure a circular rod and one end of the twisted wire in a vise. Slowly bend the twisted wire around the rod.

6 Continue to bend the twisted wire around the rod until all of the wire has been used and the wires have formed a coil.

Fastener for Thong

1 With wire snips, cut a piece of wire 10 inches long. Use the round-nosed pliers to grip one end of the wire and coil it around one side of the pliers, from the bottom and coiling upward.

2 When you have an even coil, remove the coiled wire from the pliers by slipping it over the end of the nose.

3 Use the round-nosed pliers to bend the end lengths of wire into either a loop or a hook; this will become the actual fastening.

4 To attach the leather thong to the coiled wire fastening, thread the thong through the center of the coil. Tie a knot in the end of the thong and pull the thong back so that the knot is discreetly hidden inside of the coil.

5 Finish the fastening by trimming off the excess thong using a pair of scissors.

Thongs and threads are best trimmed with scissors.

Coiled Hook and Loop Fastening

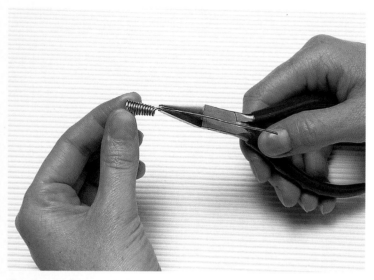

1 Cut a length of wire approximately 12 inches in length. Using a pair of round-nosed pliers, coil the wire, starting from the bottom of the pliers and working upward.

2 Using the flat-nosed pliers, bend the excess wire at 90 degrees.

3 With the round-nosed pliers, bend the wire over, forming a loop.

4 Using the tips of the round-nosed pliers, bend the wire back on itself, forming a hook.

5 Take the flat-nosed pliers and carefully manipulate the bent back wire so that it follows the first wire.

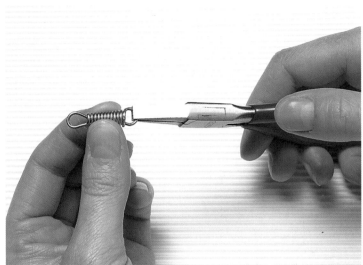

6 When the wire is satisfactorily bent, cut off the excess wire with a pair of wire snips and tuck the end discreetly into the coil.

7 At the opposite and wider end of the coil, use the flat-nosed pliers to bend the very last coil in half at 90 degrees, again making sure the end of the wire is tucked into the coil itself. This forms the mechanism by which the fastener is connected to the necklace.

The coiled hook and loop fastening provides a neat finish to the Leather and Fine Copper necklace (page 152).

Coiled Loop Fastening

1 Cut a piece of wire approximately 10 inches in length. Using a pair of round-nosed pliers, coil the wire, starting from the bottom of the pliers and working upward.

2 Continue to coil the wire along the length of the nose of the pliers, keeping the growing coil tight and even.

3 Remove the tapering coil from the pliers and use the excess straight wire to form a loop.

4 The loop is created by bending the wire over on itself and tucking the end into the coil. This forms the fastening mechanism.

5 At the opposite and wider end of the coil, use the flat-nosed pliers to bend the very last coil in half at 90 degrees, again making sure that the end of the wire is tucked into the coil. This forms the mechanism by which the fastener is connected to the necklace.

Single Wire Hook Fastener

1 Cut a length of wire approximately 9 inches in length. Use the round-nosed pliers to coil the wire around one and a half times.

2 Holding the coils between your fingers, bend the wire in a large loop with the aid of the round-nosed pliers.

3 To finish the hook fastening, cut off the excess wire with the wire snips.

Single Wire Loop Fastener

1 Cut a length of wire approximately 9 inches in length. Use the round-nosed pliers to coil the wire around one and a half times.

2 Holding the coils between your fingers, bend the wire in a large loop with the aid of the round-nosed pliers.

3 To finish the fastener, cut the wire where the loop comes around full circle. Make sure this loop is larger than the first coil to ensure easy fastening.

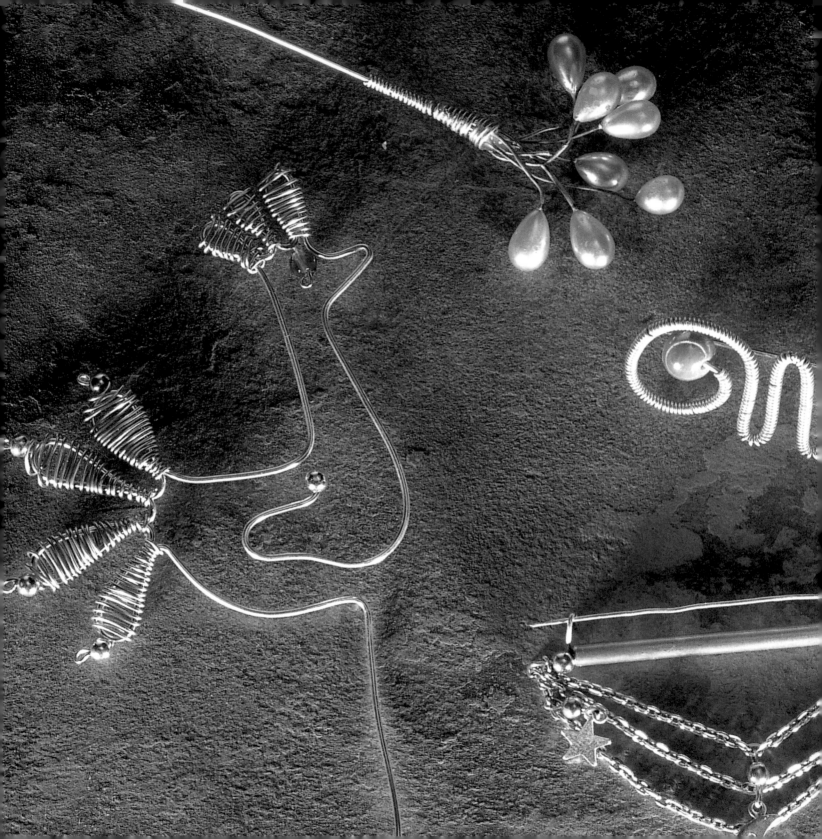

wire

Dog and Bone Bracelet

Fun and jolly, but it still looks quite classic. You can make lots of variations—simply let your imagination run wild!

YOU WILL NEED

round-nosed pliers

24 inches of 14-gauge metal wire

flat-nosed pliers

wire cutters

coil of very fine metal wire

seventeen jump rings

two fasteners

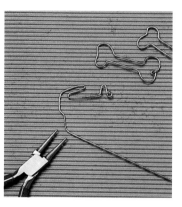

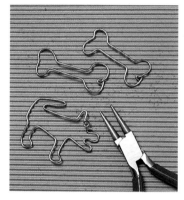

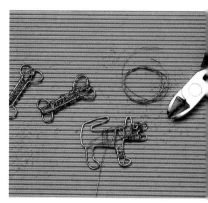

1 Shape two bones, each with 6 inches of the wire, then bend a small circle in the remaining wire (the dog's eye), and continue to bend into a dog outline as above.

2 Once your dog shape is complete, make a loop in the end of the wire. Link this through the eye and secure together. In the same way, bend and secure the ends of the bones.

3 Wrap the very fine wire around the dog and both bones, very tightly and securely, twisting any loose wire ends into a neighboring wire for safety.

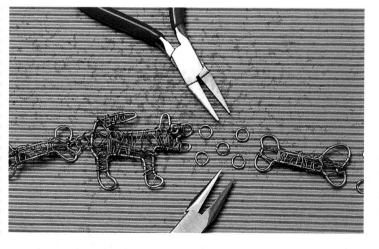

4 Fix jump rings to link together the dog and bones, then bend the shapes to fit the wrist. Attach a fastener to either end, and it is ready to wear.

Spiral Pin

Fine silver wire tightly bound around stronger silver wire enables the construction of a durable pin.

1 Bind the 14-gauge wire tightly around the 7-gauge wire. Leave at least 2½ inches of 14-gauge wire uncovered at one end and ¾ inch uncovered at the other end.

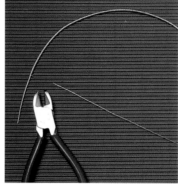

2 Thread your bead onto the shorter uncovered end and bend back the wire to secure. Cut off any excess 7-gauge wire.

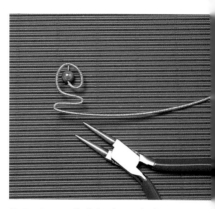

3 Begin to spiral the bound wire around the bead. Curl and twist the wire to produce an aesthetically pleasing form, until you get to within ½ inch of the uncovered 14-gauge wire.

4 Turn the piece over. Curl over the exposed 14-gauge wire to form a pin, and use the wire at the bead end to form a hook. Cut off any excess wire and file to a fine point.

Spiraled Silver Choker

Quantities of silver wire coiled tightly make a chunky close-fitting necklace with a richly textured surface quality.

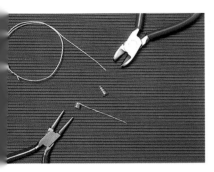  

1 Using wire snips, cut 22 lengths of silver wire, each measuring 6½ inches. Grip one end of one piece of silver wire in the round-nosed pliers and wrap it around one side of the tapering nose, starting at the bottom of the pliers and coiling upwards. Repeat on all of the lengths of wire.

2 To produce the necklace's linking system, open up the last coil at each end of the spirals, using the flat-nosed pliers, and gently bend the single loop at 90 degrees, so that it sits at right angles to the body of the spiral. Repeat.

3 Line up the coiled wires in the design of the final choker, the narrow taper facing the widest end of the next coiled section. Next, with the flat-nosed pliers, open up the bent links and thread on the next coiled section. Close the link, making sure it is secure.

YOU WILL NEED

ruler

wire snips

5 yards of 14-gauge silver wire

round-nosed pliers

flat-nosed pliers

4 Link together all of the spirals until they are fastened to one another in a chain. Finish the necklace by making and attaching an integral coiled hook and loop fastening (see page 22).

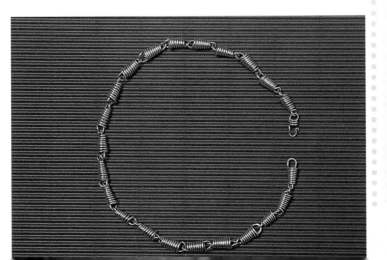

Sophisticated Silver

Contrast the clean lines of silver tubing with black leather thong
to create a discreet but modern necklace.

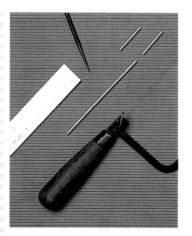

1 With a pencil, mark off the tube
into 17 separate lengths, each
measuring 1⅜ inches. With a
piercing saw, carefully cut the tube.

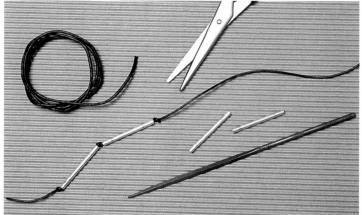

2 File both ends of the cut sections with a needle file. Tie a tight knot 1½
inches from one end of the leather thong and thread on one section of the
silver tube. Tie another knot close to the other end of the tube to secure it
in place on the thong. Repeat this process of threading the tube and tying
knots until all of the sections of tube have been used.

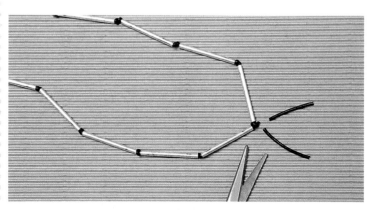

3 To finish, tie the two ends of the
thong together securely. Finally,
cut off any excess lengths of thong.

Wires and Washers

Household washers have been wrapped with wire and linked together to produce attractive drop earrings.

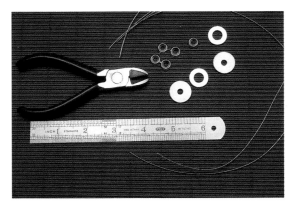

1 Measure and cut the following lengths of wire:
- two 12-inch lengths
- two 8-inch lengths
- two 7-inch lengths

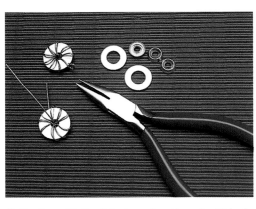

2 Starting with the ¾-inch washer, thread a 12-inch length of wire through the central hole and bind it around the washer. Twist the excess wire at the starting point and curl around to form a loop. Repeat with the other ¾-inch washer

3 Wrap a ⅞-inch washer with an 8-inch length of wire, which also holds a screw cup washer. Tuck the ends of the wire into the middle hole. Repeat.

YOU WILL NEED

ruler

wire cutters

54 inches of 10-gauge brass wire

two ¾-inch diameter (¼-inch center hole) washers

half-round pliers

two ⅞-inch diameter (⅜-inch center hole) washers

four No. 6 screw cup brass washers

six jump rings

two earring hooks

4 Finally, bind a 7-inch length of wire around each of the remaining screw cup washers.

5 Link the three sections together with jump rings.

6 Attach an earring hook to the top twisted loop of wire to complete the earrings.

Silver Wire Flowers

Silver is a material that is easy to manipulate; however, you could experiment with other metals such as copper or brass wire and have contrasting color effects.

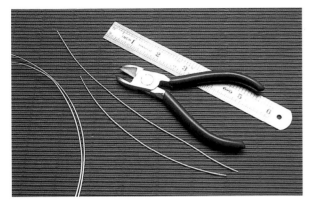

1 Measure and cut the following:
two 8-inch lengths and
two 6-inch lengths of
14-gauge silver wire
two 4-inch lengths of 10-gauge
silver wire.

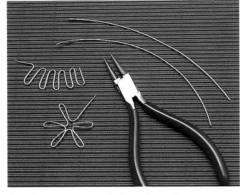

2 Using round-nosed pliers, form the 14-gauge wire pieces into an even zigzag pattern. Then, bend the wire around to form the "petals" of the flower. Leave ½ inch of wire unformed on the end of each flower.

3 When complete, hammer the flowers to flatten and slightly texture their surface.

YOU WILL NEED

ruler

wire cutters

28 inches of 14-gauge round section sterling silver wire

8 inches of 10-gauge round section sterling silver wire

round-nosed pliers

hammer

flat needle file

four silver jump rings

4 With round-nosed pliers, form a central spiral in each flower from the remaining ½ inch of wire.

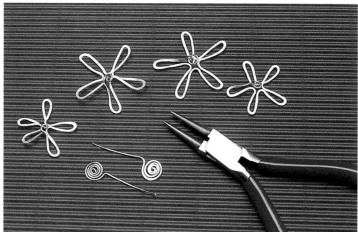

5 Using the 10-gauge lengths of wire, form spirals, leaving 1 inch unformed. Hammer the spirals flat. Then, bend the remaining wire into a hook.

6 Using a flat needle file, file the ends of the hooks smooth.

7 Assemble the earrings using four jump rings, two for each, to connect the flowers and hooks together.

Folded Brass and Glass

This simple yet bold neckpiece uses contrasting brass wire and black beads to create a rhythmic folded wire necklace.

YOU WILL NEED

ruler

wire snips

4 yards of 14-gauge brass wire

round-nosed pliers

hammer

protective gloves

ten flat round glass beads

two pairs flat-nosed pliers

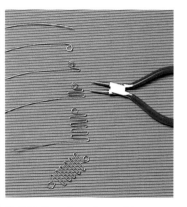

1 With the wire snips, cut ten 12-inch lengths of brass wire. Make loops on the ends of each length of wire, using a pair of round-nosed pliers. Then, take the pliers and bend the wire back and forth on itself to produce an undulating pattern approximately 1 inch wide. Repeat the process until nearly all of the wire has been used up. Finish by making another connecting loop with the round-nosed pliers.

2 Using a hammer, tap the wires gently on a firm surface so that they become flattened. Wear protective gloves while hammering the wire.

3 Using wire snips, cut ten 1-inch lengths of brass wire. Using the round-nosed pliers, make a loop at one end of the wire. Gently tap the looped wires on a firm surface to flatten them.

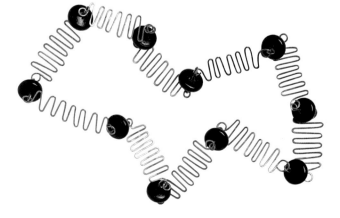

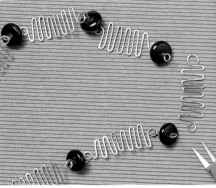

4 Thread a glass bead onto each short wire and, with a pair of round-nosed pliers, make a loop at the other end of the wire to secure the bead.

5 Using two pairs of flat-nosed pliers, open up the loops of all the sections and connect the loops together, in the sequence shown, to form the necklace.

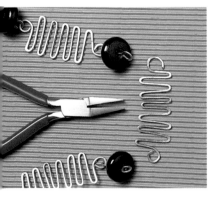

6 Close the loops with the flat-nosed pliers, making sure that all of the linked loops are securely fastened together.

Fantasy Bird

This elegant silver wire pin was inspired by exotic birds from South America.

YOU WILL NEED

32 inches of 14-gauge silver wire

half round pliers

round-nosed pliers

wire cutters

36 inches of 7-gauge silver wire

one ⅛-inch blue glass bead

five ⅛-inch silver-plated beads

needle file

pin stopper

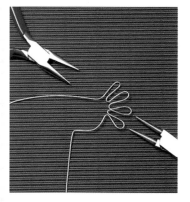

1 Using the 14-gauge silver wire, leave a pin about 3 inches long at one end, then begin to bend the body of a bird, working toward the tail with the round-nosed pliers.

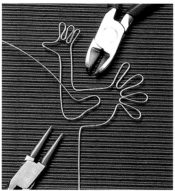

2 Complete the shape of your bird and cut off any excess wire.

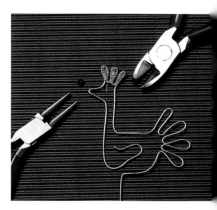

3 Bind some of the 7-gauge wire around the comb of the bird. Leave enough wire to thread on and secure the blue glass bead just above the beak, to make an eye.

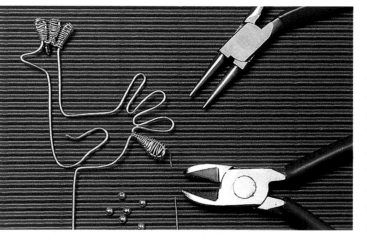

4 Bind the rest of the 7-gauge wire around the tail feathers, leaving spare ends of wire at the tail tips. Thread four of the silver beads onto the tail tips, then loop the wire to complete. Thread a bead onto the loop of the bird wing. Cut and file the pin and put the pin stopper on the end.

Precious Wire and Beads

Using a weaving method traditionally reserved for wool, you will be pleasantly surprised by the results.

1 To make a bobbin, drill a hole approximately 2 inches in diameter through a chunky piece of wood.

2 With a pen, evenly make five marks as shown.

3 Where marked, securely screw in the five miniature screws. Your bobbin is now complete.

4 Thread approximately 25 beads onto your wire.

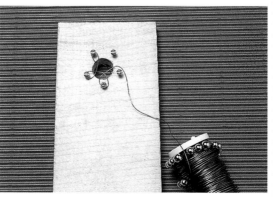

5 Loop the wire around your bobbin as shown.

YOU WILL NEED

chunky piece of wood

drill

pen

five miniature screws

screwdriver

coil of very fine metal wire

metal beads or small colored glass beads

flat-nosed pliers

wire cutters

two jump rings

two fasteners

6 Continue to loop your wire, lifting the lower loop up and over the top loop each time with your flat-nosed pliers.

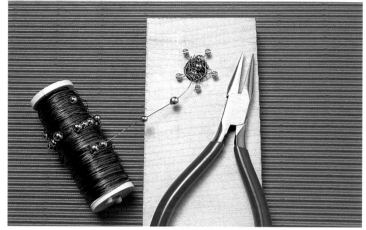

7 Gradually add the beads, by sliding them down the wire while you continue to loop as before. Although the process is very slow, the results are rewarding and the finished product is delightful.

8 Your length of bracelet should emerge from the underside of the bobbin. Just continue looping and lifting, and adding the beads, until the bracelet is the length you desire. You could also make many lengths and fasten them to each other on the wrist.

9 Secure a jump ring and fastener to each end, so they can be linked when you wear the bracelet.

Braided Silver Choker

Fine silver wires braided together create a delicate yet elegant close-fitting necklace.

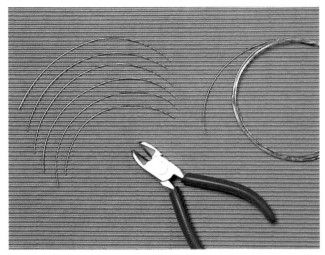

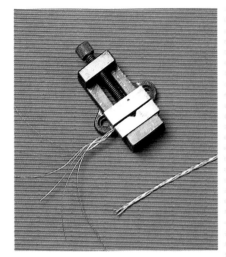

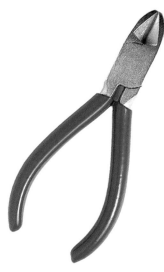

1 Loosely place a length of string around the neck and measure the length of the string. This will act as a guide for the size of choker. Add an extra 2½ inches to this. Using the total measurement, cut six lengths of the silver wire with wire snips.

2 Group the wires into three sets of two wires and place the ends of all six wires in a vise; make sure they are secure. Braid these three sets until all of the wires are braided together.

3 Remove the wires from the vise and use two pairs of flat-nosed pliers to twist the ends of the braided wires together. To do this, hold the wires 1 inch from the end with one pair of pliers and, using the other pair, slowly twist the ends together. Do this at both ends to secure the wires.

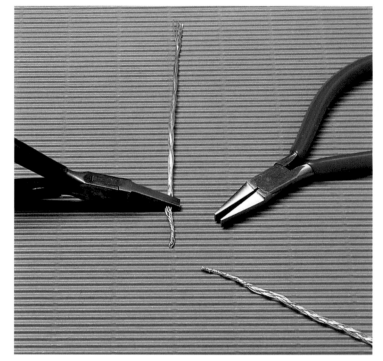

4 The fastening for this choker is an integral part of the neckpiece (the twisted end sections become the fastening). With the round-nosed pliers, bend one end of the wires around until it forms a hook. For the other end, take a longer length and bend the wires until they form a loop. Then, twist the excess wires of the loop around the main body of the necklace, securing the loop in place. Flatten any sharp wires that are protruding. Finally, gently bend the braided wires to form a circle using your hands.

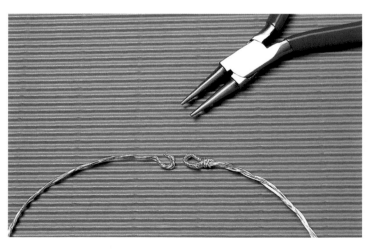

Textured Silver

· ·

Textured wires manipulated in a lively manner and combined with gold glass beads create a flamboyant close-fitting necklace.

YOU WILL NEED

pencil

paper

ruler

45 inches of 18-gauge silver wire

wire snips

round-nosed pliers

flat-nosed pliers

hammer

ten gold barrel glass beads

1 With a pencil and a piece of paper, draw the undulating shape, 2½ inches long. Allow for a loop at both ends. This will become the template for the wire components. Cut ten 2½ inch lengths of silver wire with wire snips. Using the round-nosed pliers, manipulate the wires to the shape on the piece of paper, following it as a template. Make a loop at one end of each wire with the pliers.

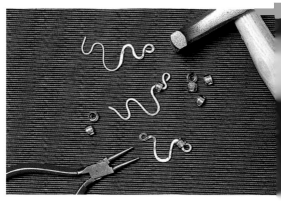

2 Hammer the wires until they are heavily textured. Slide a glass bead on one end and, with round-nosed pliers, make a loop at the other end of the wire.

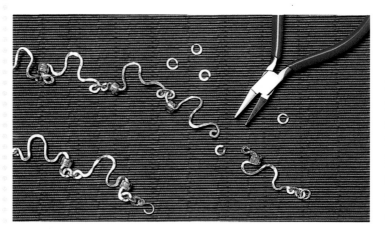

3 Make 14 silver wire jump rings (see page 19). Texture, by tapping with a hammer. Thread them through the loops in the bent wire, linking the sections with the flat-nosed pliers. Attach the coiled hook and loop fastening with the remaining jump rings.

Free-Form Wire Brooch

One continuous length of silver wire is decorated with beads and twisted to create an abstract form.

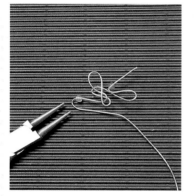

1 Leaving a ¾-inch straight piece of wire at the start, begin to curl and bend the remainder of the silver wire into an interesting form.

2 Thread the beads as you go to give an even spread throughout the design.

3 Having produced the final design, curl back the remaining wire to form the pin and cut to the right length. Use the ¾ inch of wire at the opposite side of the brooch to make a safety hook.

4 File a fine point for the pin, then gently hammer the pin with the nylon mallet.

Pearl Stick Pin

Silver wire and imitation pearls create a pin inspired by natural forms.

YOU WILL NEED

6 inches of 7-gauge silver wire

round-nosed pliers

5 inches of 14-gauge silver wire

wire cutters

resin-based glue

eight teardrop pearls on stems

needle file

pin stopper

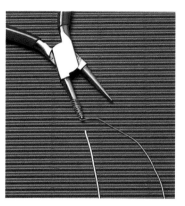

1 Bind the 7-gauge silver wire tightly around one point of the round-nosed pliers to form a cone shape.

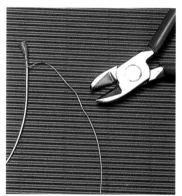

2 Take the cone and, using the rest of the wire, bind the cone tightly onto the 14-gauge wire until it is secure. Cut off any excess.

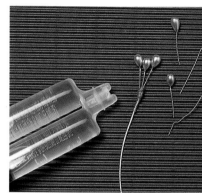

3 Fill the cone of 7-gauge wire with resin-based glue. Push the pearls into the cone and allow the glue to set.

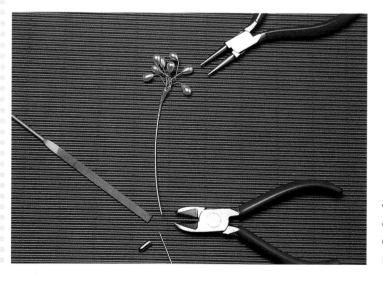

4 Curl and twist the pearls to create an interesting arrangement. Cut and file the pin to a fine point. Place a pin stopper at the end.

Moon and Stars Medal

This pin is formed from loops of chain with a moon and stars motif.

YOU WILL NEED

9 inches of 7-gauge silver wire

round-nosed pliers

1¾ inches of 28-gauge brass tube

two ⅛-inch silver beads

three silver-plated chains,
2½-inch, 3-inch, 3½-inch

needle file

two ¼-inch silver stars

½-inch silver crescent moon

three ⅛-inch gold-plated beads

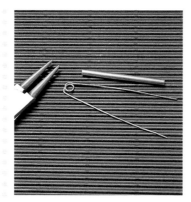

1 Take 4 inches of the silver wire and fold it in half, curling it over in the center to create a simple spring. Thread half the wire through the tube, leaving half outside to form the pin. Use the excess wire on the other end to form the safety hook.

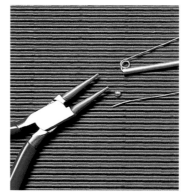

2 Take 2¾ inches of the remaining silver wire, thread a silver bead onto the end, loop, then thread this length of wire through the tube. Thread the second bead onto the wire where it protrudes from the tube. Loop and cut off the excess wire.

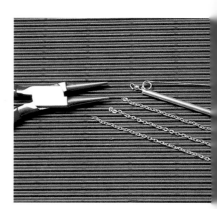

3 Open the loops of wire at the ends of the tube. Thread the chains onto the loops. Push the loops tightly together so the chains are secure. File any rough edges.

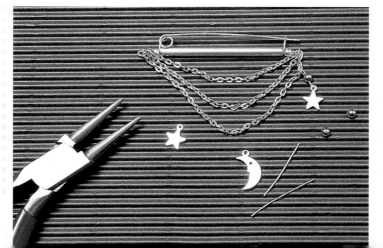

4 Take three ¾-inch lengths of the remaining silver wire and loop the stars and moon onto the separate lengths. Thread a gold bead on to each of the lengths, and loop all three onto the longest chain.

Chain Mail

What a rewarding bracelet to make! Few metalworking skills are required, but patience is a must. This bracelet should last a lifetime—why not make it from a precious metal?

lots and lots of jump rings—the quantity required depends on the size of the rings—you can always make more

two pairs flat-nosed pliers

pipe cleaner

two fasteners

1 Simply line three jump rings next to one another as shown. The jump rings become the links in this bracelet.

2 Thread a jump ring through two of the neighboring links to join them together, then close with pliers. Repeat with another ring on the other side, so that you will now have five rings linked uniformly together.

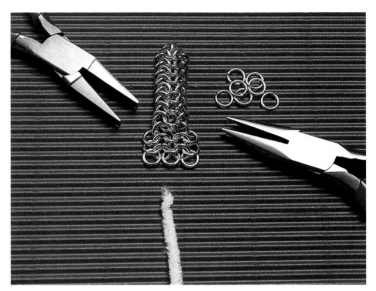

3 Onto this row, link three jump rings as in Step 1. When placed onto a flat surface, they should lie parallel to the first row of rings.

4 Repeat the process in Step 2 and continue in this manner until the bracelet is about 3 inches long.

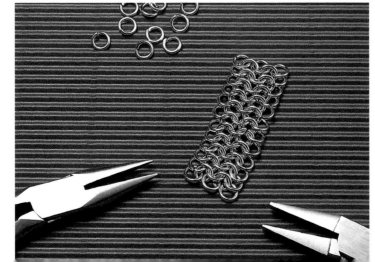

5 The formation of the links should appear very uniform and the bracelet be very flexible. Place the bracelet on a flat surface.

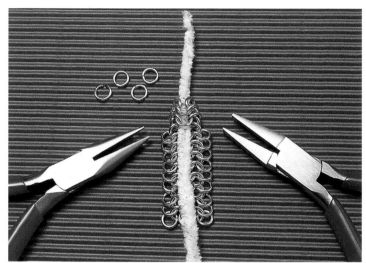

6 At this stage, you will find a pipe cleaner very useful! Keep a close eye on following the pattern you are making with the rings. Put a jump ring through the top two side links and insert the pipe cleaner. Take a second jump ring and thread it through the first, laying it flat on the pipe cleaner. Thread it through the same two side links as above. Close the jump ring with your flat-nosed pliers.

7 Repeat the process of connecting a jump ring to the flat link above it, and then to the two side links. The joins should look uniform and appear the same as the rest of the rings in the bracelet. Continue until you can wrap the bracelet comfortably around your wrist.

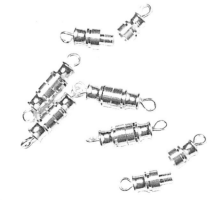

8 Add a jump ring and fastener at either end to complete this chain-mail bracelet.

Clock Piece

Broken clock and watch mechanisms can be reconstituted
to make an unusual brooch.

clock and watch pieces

resin-based glue

half round pliers

wire cutters

2 inches of 14-gauge silver wire

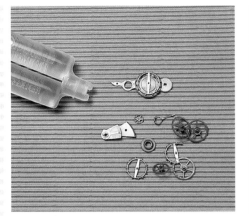

1 Select some interesting pieces of watch
mechanisms and assemble them in an
attractive form, making sure that the piece
at the end has a hole in it for attaching the
hook. Glue together and allow to set.

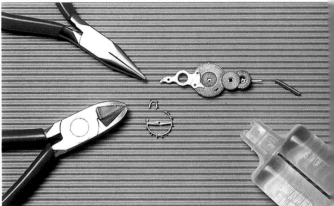

2 Cut out a small piece from a wheel, leaving most of the
circle intact, curl it to make a hook shape, and glue it into the
hole in the end section of the completed design. Take a length
of clock spring and glue this to the opposite end.

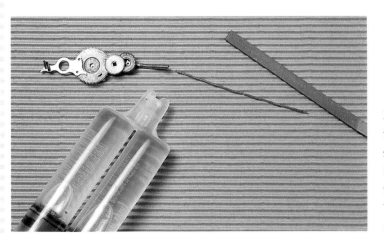

3 Glue the piece of silver wire into
the spring and allow the glue to
set. Cut the wire to fit along the
back of the brooch so it reaches
the hook. File to a fine point.
The spring should keep the pin
under tension.

sheet
plastic, and paper

Copper Star Pendant

Simple sheet metal texturing techniques have been used in conjunction with glass beads to create this bold, fun star pendant.

YOU WILL NEED

pen

3½ x 3½-inch piece of thin copper sheet metal

tin snips

protective gloves

needle file

center punch

hammer

hand drill

round-nosed pliers

flat-nosed pliers

three glass beads

two copper jump rings

bead wire

34 inches of black leather thong

1 Draw a star shape on the copper sheet and then cut it out with the tin snips. Make sure you wear a pair of gloves when cutting the metal to protect your hands from the metal's sharp edges.

2 File the star and tap the surface with a hammer to create texture. Place the shape on a wooden surface. Using a center punch and a hammer, tap the back of the star to create a raised pattern.

3 Drill a hole in one of the points of the star. Open up a jump ring, slide it through the hole, and then close it. Use another jump ring to attach the star's jump ring to a bead wire.

4 Slide the beads onto the wire and make a loop with the round-nosed pliers to secure. Fasten the thong around the loop and knot the two ends together to secure.

Aluminum Button Brooch

A button cover is used to hold folded aluminum gauze to fashion a rosette effect.

1 Draw around the back of the button cover on the center of the aluminum gauze.

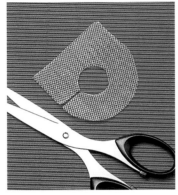

2 Cut out this marked center using scissors. Then, cut away the outside corners to make a more circular shape.

3 Spray the outside of the button cover with gold paint, following the manufacturer's instructions.

YOU WILL NEED

marker

1-inch metal button cover

3-inch square of aluminum gauze

scissors

gold spray paint

round-nosed pliers

half round pliers

gold pen

brooch back

resin-based glue

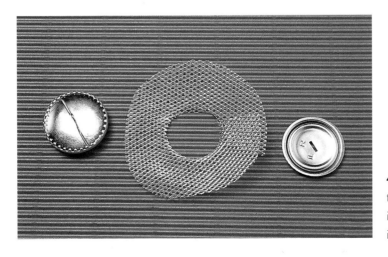

4 Overlap the gauze to make sure that the hole is the right size to fit in the button cover. Trap the gauze inside the cover.

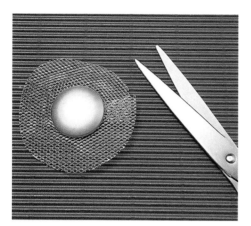

5 Cut the gauze to an even shape.

6 Roll over the outer edges of the gauze with the round-nosed pliers to make them durable and safe for skin and clothing. Then, make the edges flat by pressing them down with the half round pliers.

7 Use the half round pliers to slightly pleat the gauze to make a frill. Draw a border round the edge with the gold pen.

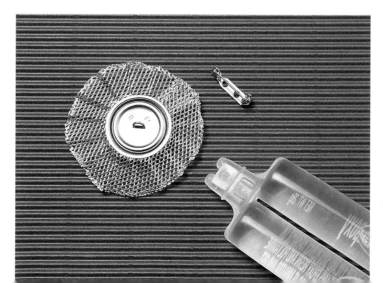

8 Glue on the brooch back with the resin-based glue.

Celtic-style Pin

Here is a hammer-textured brass and copper pin inspired by Celtic knots.

1 Clean the metal with wire wool. Draw two spiral shapes onto paper and then lightly glue one onto the copper sheet and one onto the brass sheet.

2 Saw-pierce the shapes out of the metal sheets, following your paper template and cutting through the paper at the same time. Remove the paper and then file the rough edges of the metal spirals.

3 Use the chasing hammer to create a textured effect on the copper and brass spirals by hammering the flat metal.

YOU WILL NEED

3 x 2- inch pieces of thin brass and copper sheet

wire wool

pen

paper

resin-based glue

piercing saw and size 0 saw blade

needle file

chasing hammer

round-nosed pliers

4¾ inches of 18-gauge copper wire

decorative bead with ¹⁄₁₆-inch hole

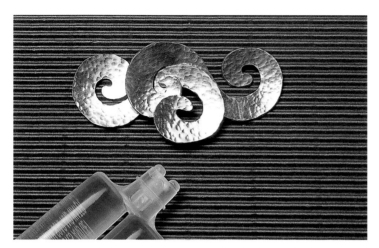

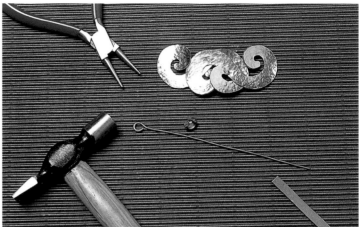

4 Interlock the two spirals to create a pattern. Bend back the outside edge spirals so that the center of the piece arches slightly. Use a little resin glue at the back to hold the pieces in place.

5 Curl the top of the copper wire to form a loop and hammer it flat. Thread on the bead so it is close to the loop. File the other end of the copper wire to a fine point.

6 Thread the wire in through the top spiral and out again through the bottom. This will attach the pin securely to the garment.

Enameled Brooch

Enamel paints are used to create bright color on a metal surface.

1 Draw a template for a 2½-inch diameter disc with tabs on the cardboard as shown. Clean the copper with the wire wool. Use the template to mark the shape onto the copper. Cut out using tin snips.

2 Using the saw, cut a 1½-inch diameter circle from the center.

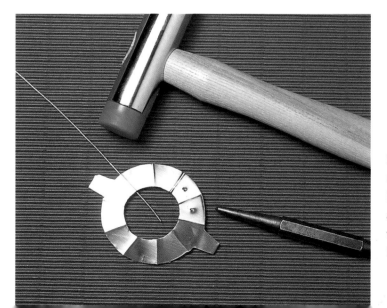

3 Hammer the sheet with the nylon mallet over the wire to make indentations in a regular pattern around the brooch. Intersperse with center-punch marks on the back to make a pattern.

YOU WILL NEED

marker

cardboard

scissors

3¼ x 3¼ inches of thin copper sheet

wire wool

tin snips

piercing saw

center punch

nylon mallet

round-nosed pliers

5 inches of 14-gauge silver wire

half round pliers

wire cutters

needle file

paintbrush

orange and turquoise enamel paints

4 With the round-nosed pliers, roll one of the flaps over to the back to make a tiny tube. Fold the second flap over and gently curl down its corners. Thread the wire through the tube and fold it back over the tube with the half round pliers to secure it in place. Bend the longer length of the wire to fit across the back of the brooch. Cut to size to enable it to hook under the flap. File to a fine point.

5 Use the enamel paints to color the sections of the brooch. These will give the brooch extra definition and sparkle. Do not paint over the edges. If necessary, lightly clean the raised ridges and center-punch marks to highlight the copper, using the wire wool.

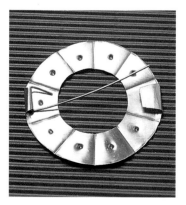

6 When the paint is dry, clean the back of the brooch and file away any rough edges.

Golden Triangles

These glamorous golden earrings are made from inexpensive and recycled materials.
String is used to create a raised surface pattern.

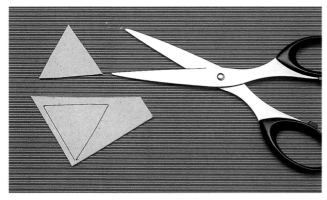

1 Draw and cut out two triangle shapes from thick cardboard. Try to keep the edges equal in length and do not make the triangles too large for you to wear comfortably on your ears.

2 Apply a layer of torn pieces of paper with PVA or wallpaper paste. Cover both sides of the triangles entirely. Allow to dry for 30 to 40 minutes.

3 Attach three 3-inch lengths of string with glue to the inside edges of both triangles to form an inner triangular pattern. Allow to dry and then trim off any excess string.

YOU WILL NEED

pen

4 x 2-inch cardboard

scissors

scrap paper

PVA glue or wallpaper adhesive

paintbrush

12 inches of string

gold foil-type wrapping paper or candy wrapper

blue foil-type wrapping paper or candy wrapper

clear varnish

earring stems and backs

resin-based glue

4 Cover the triangles with glue and place a sheet of gold paper on top of each. Carefully smooth down the paper to define the surface pattern. Fold the gold paper around the triangles to cover the backs and trim off any excess paper if necessary.

5 Cut a small triangle of blue paper foil and glue into the center of each triangle. Following the manufacturer's directions, apply a coat of clear varnish all over the triangles in a well-ventilated area. Allow to dry for six hours.

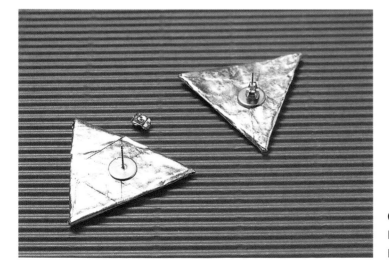

6 Attach earring stems to the backs of the earrings with resin-based glue to complete them.

Acetate Fan

A color photocopy on an acetate surface gives strength and durability and creates an easy-to-make and attractive piece of jewelry.

YOU WILL NEED

ruler

8½ x 11-inch color copy of an interesting design on acetate

scissors

8½ x 11-inch sheet of white paper

6 inches of 7-gauge silver wire

⅛-inch silver-plated bead

flat-nosed pliers

wire cutters

needle file

3½ inches of 14-gauge nickel wire

resin-based glue

pin stopper

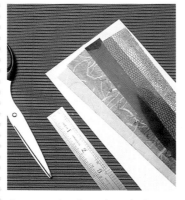

1 Cut a strip of acetate 8 inches long by 1 inch wide. Cut the strip in half to make two 4-inch strips.

2 Sandwich a strip of 3¾ x ¾-inch white paper between the two acetate strips to allow a small border all the way around. Fold the strips to form an accordion.

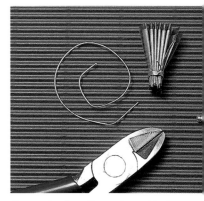

3 Use the fine silver wire to bind the accordion together at one end. Thread on the silver-plated bead and secure by squeezing the wire flat with the flat-nosed pliers. Cut off the excess.

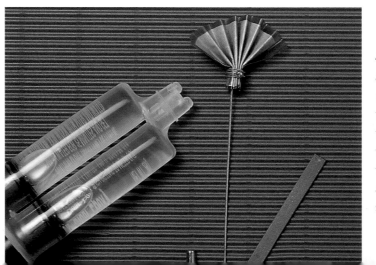

4 Open up the other end of the accordion to form a fan. File a point on the nickel wire and, using the resin-based glue, stick it inside the bottom of the fan and allow it to set. Use the left-over silver wire to bind around the base of the fan and down the pin. Put the pin stopper on the end.

Embossed Copper Brooch

This is a copper foil brooch with a hand-drawn motif, using gentle heat to color.

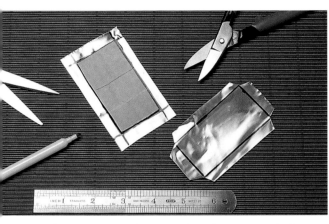

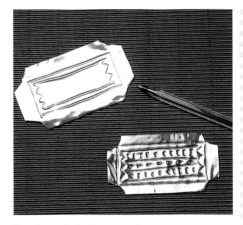

YOU WILL NEED

marker pen

ruler

tin snips

3½ x 2 inches of copper foil

ballpoint pen

flat-nosed pliers

gas flame torch

1½ x 3 inches of cardboard

scissors

PVA glue

1¼ x 2¾ inches of felt

resin-based glue

brooch back

1 Using the cardboard as a template, draw a 1½ x 3 inch rectangle onto the copper foil, extending the lines to the edge of the sheet. Cut away the corners of the copper to the edge of the template.

2 Using a ballpoint pen, draw a pattern on the surface of the copper foil. You will need to press quite hard.

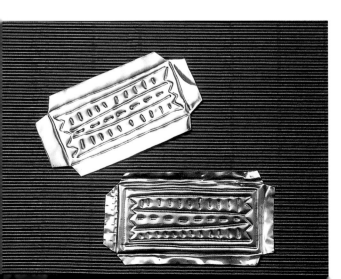

3 Using flat-nosed pliers, hold the copper sheet over a very gentle flame (a gas stove will do). Keep taking the metal to and from the heat until the metal changes color. Allow the metal to cool before touching it.

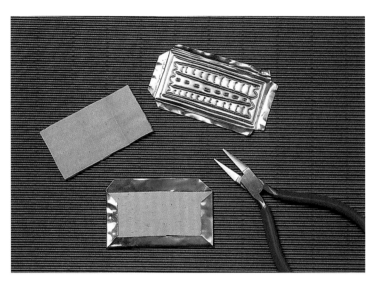

4 Place the rectangle of cardboard on the back of the cooled metal and fold the copper edges around the card to secure it.

5 Use PVA glue to stick the felt to the back of the card and over the copper edges.

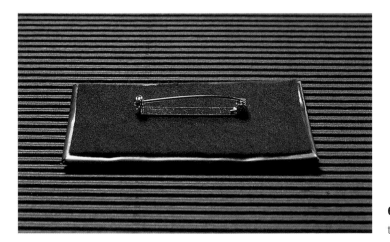

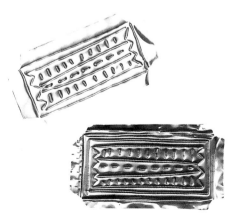

6 Finally, use the resin-based glue to attach a brooch back to the felt.

Punched Metal Brooch

Use punching to create pattern and texture around a simply constructed setting for a stone.

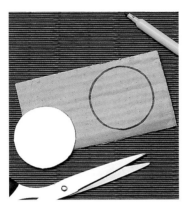

1 Cut out a 2-inch diameter circle and 1¾-inch diameter circle from the cardboard.

2 Clean the metal with the wire wool. Use the templates to mark the circles on the metal, the larger onto the aluminum sheet, the smaller on to the brass. Cut the circles out of the metal using the tin snips. Protect your hands from the sharp edges with the gloves.

YOU WILL NEED

marker

5 x 4 inches of cardboard

scissors

2 x 2-inch thick aluminum sheet

1¾ x 1¾-inch thin brass sheet

wire wool

tin snips

protective gloves

center punch

hammer

½-inch diameter flat back glass stone

1¼ x 1¼-inch brass shim

resin-based glue

brooch back

3 Use the center punch to create an indented pattern around the edge of both circles and lines coming in to the center of the brass circle (three punch marks for each line is enough).

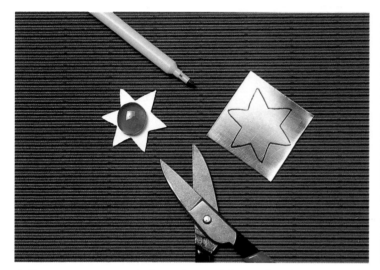

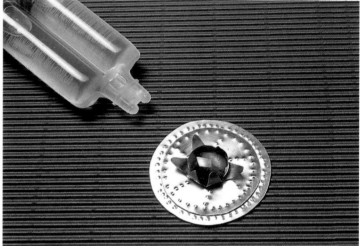

4 Place your stone onto the brass sheet and draw a six-point star around it. Each point should be about ⅜ inch from the edge of the stone. Cut out the star with snips, taking care not to cut yourself on the sharp edges.

5 Use the resin-based glue to join the aluminum and brass circles together. Wrap the points of the brass star around the stone, which should hold it in place. Glue the stone in its setting to the center of the brass circle and allow the glue to set.

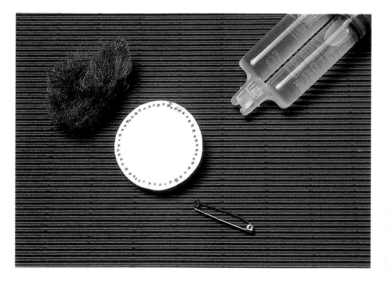

6 Finally, clean the back of the brooch with the wire wool and use resin-based glue to attach the brooch back.

Chain-linked Brooch

Colorful plasticized material linked by chains and bells makes a pretty double-sided brooch.

YOU WILL NEED

scissors

two different color sticks of modeling plastic

gas flame

six silver-plated bells

drill and 1/16-inch drill bit

flat-nosed pliers

half round pliers

three lengths of 3½-inch silver-plated chain

two silver jump rings

resin-based glue

two round brooch backs

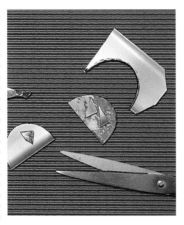

1 Cut out two half-circles from one of the modeling plastics. Cut small pieces from the other plastic, lay them on the half-circles, and heat the plastics gently with a flame until they melt together.

2 Drill holes at the top of each semi-circle's arc. Then thread two bells onto each length of chain.

3 Loop the jump rings through the holes in the two half-circles. Lay the chains between them and hook them onto the jump rings. Close the rings tightly to secure the chains.

4 Turn the pieces over and glue one brooch back to each semi-circle, using the resin-based glue.

Brass and Glass Domes

This project utilizes a simple stone setting method with a glass dome as the "stone." Patterns have been scored into the base plate which can be varied in shape or pattern to your own design.

1 Draw around your domed beads with a pen onto the brass sheet. Sketch a star shape of about eight points around each circle, depending upon the size of your dome. These will form the "claws" to hold your stone in place.

2 Cut out the two stars with tin snips. Remove the very ends of the points so that they are not dangerously sharp.

3 Place a small amount of the resin-based glue in the center of the stars and put the glass domes in position. Leave to dry for 20 minutes.

YOU WILL NEED

pen

two glass domed beads

6 x 2 inches thin brass sheet

tin snips

resin-based glue

flat needle file

wire wool

two earring clip findings or stems and backs

4 When the adhesive has set, bend up the points of the stars to enclose the domes.

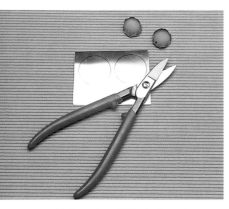

5 Draw two 1½-inch diameter circles onto the remaining brass sheet. Cut out with tin snips.

6 File the edges and clean the metal surface with wire wool. Draw lines ½ inch long all around the edge of each circle with the pen.

7 Glue the stone setting to the center of the base circle with resin-based glue. Leave to set until fully hardened.

8 Attach an earring clip fitting or posts for pierced ears to the back of each base plate with resin-based glue.

Copper Leaves

Combine a thin copper sheet with wire to produce intriguing leafy earrings.

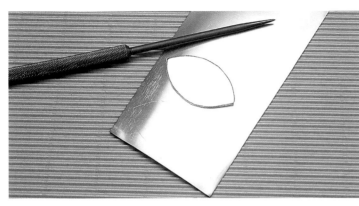

1 Cut out a leaf shape template from the cardstock. Draw around it with a metal scriber or pen onto the copper sheet twice.

2 Using tin snips, cut out the two leaf shapes.

YOU WILL NEED

thin cardstock

scissors

metal scriber or pen

3 x 2½ inches of thin copper sheet

tin snips

drill and ⅟₃₂-inch drill bit

13 inches of 14-gauge round section copper wire

wire cutters

round-nosed pliers

ruler (or straightedge)

hammer

center punch

nylon mallet

two earring hooks

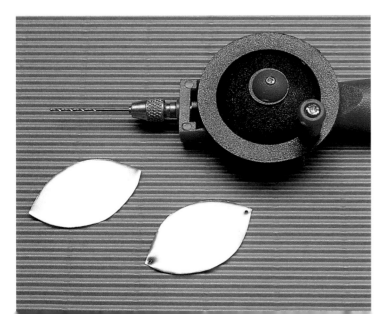

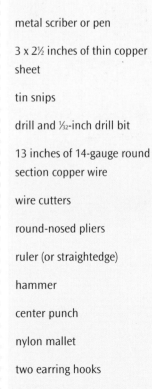

3 Drill a small hole into the top and bottom points of each of the leaf shapes.

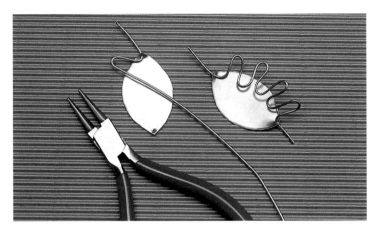

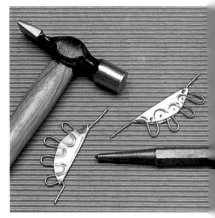

4 Cut two 6½-inch lengths of copper wire. Insert one end of one piece of the wire into each leaf, leaving 1 inch protruding from the top. Using round-nosed pliers, form a zigzag pattern with the wire. Push the other end of the wire through the remaining hole. Repeat the process with the second leaf and wire.

5 Place a ruler (or straightedge) across the leaf as a guide and fold in half with the wire pattern remaining on the outside of the leaf. Repeat with the second leaf.

6 Using a center punch and hammer, punch dots between the wire pattern. Next gently hammer the metal surface with a nylon mallet to define the patterns.

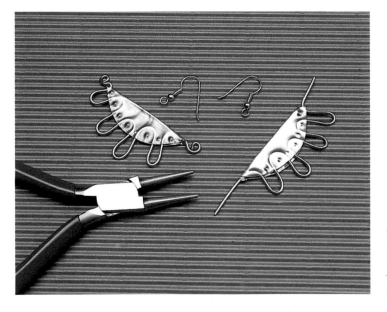

7 Form a spiral using round-nosed pliers on the ends of the wire. Attach earring hooks to the top spiral to complete.

Saw-pierced Motifs

Here, intricate saw-pierced motifs are linked together. Templates could be enlarged to make bigger versions of one image or small dainty earrings could consist of a single motif.

1 Draw bird, flower, and heart shapes onto the card, then cut out to form templates.

2 Cover the pieces of silver and brass with masking tape.

3 Use the card templates to draw: two birds and two flowers on the silver sheet; two hearts and two flowers on the brass sheet.

4 Drill large center holes into the flowers. Remember to center punch before attempting to drill any holes. Next, drill small holes at the top and bottom into the birds, hearts, and silver flowers. The remaining brass flowers require only one hole at the top.

YOU WILL NEED

pen

cardstock

scissors

2 x 2½ inches of thin sterling silver sheet

2 x 2 inches of thin brass sheet

masking tape

drill

small ⅟₃₆ inch and ⅟₁₆ inch drill bits

center punch

piercing saw frame and 2/0 saw blades

wire wool

flat needle file

eight jump rings

two earring hooks

5 Saw-pierce the shapes from the silver and brass sheets.

6 Remove the masking tape and file the edges. Clean the metal surface with wire wool to bring up the shine.

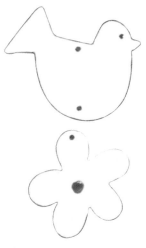

7 Link the shapes together with jump rings through the drilled holes and attach earring hooks to finish.

Aluminum and Fabric Discs

For this project, we have combined metal with fabric. You could make these earrings using a particular color in the center to match an outfit. If you are unable to obtain the textured aluminum, hammer sheet aluminum to create a similar effect.

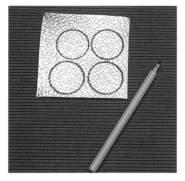

1 Draw two 1½-inch and two 1¼-inch diameter circles on the aluminum sheet with the compass.

2 Using a piercing saw, cut out the aluminum circles.

3 Draw 1-inch diameter circles in the center of the larger discs.

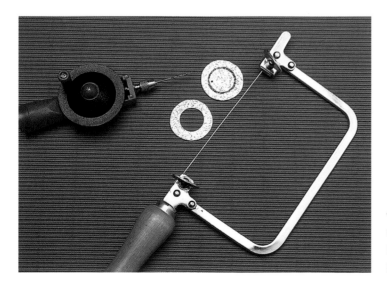

4 Drill a small hole near the edge of the inner circle, insert the saw blade, and pierce out the centers of both discs.

YOU WILL NEED

compass

pen

7 x 2 inches of textured aluminum sheet

piercing saw frame and 2/0 saw blades

drill

small ⅟₃₂-inch drill bit

half round file

flat needle file

emery paper

fabric for center

scissors

stuffing

strong, clear adhesive

resin-based glue

four small clips

two earring stems and backs

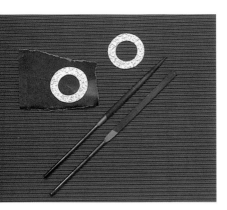

5 Smooth both edges of the discs using files and emery paper.

6 Cut out two 1¼-inch diameter circles of fabric.

7 Put a tiny ball of stuffing into the center of the fabric circle and apply a small amount of clear adhesive or PVA to secure in place. Put the fabric on top of the disc with the center removed.

8 Glue on the backing circle of aluminum with resin-based glue, thus sandwiching the fabric between the metal. Hold together with clips until the glue has set. Attach stem fittings to the backs to finish the earrings.

Textured Brass

Bold brass geometric shapes, textured to create an antique feel and assembled in a strong pattern, contribute to fashion a necklace which has echoes of ancient Mexican civilizations.

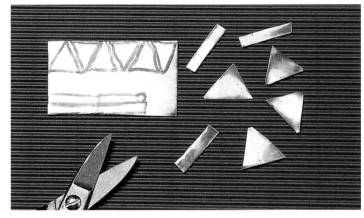

1 With a pen, draw ten triangular shapes approximately ⅞ x ⅞ inches in size and also 13 rectangles 1⅛ x ¼ inches on the brass sheet. Keep the shapes roughly the same sizes. Wearing protective gloves use the tin snips to cut out the drawn shapes.

2 Gently tap the surface of the metal shapes with a hammer until they are textured all over. It might be necessary to wear gloves to hold the metal shapes while hammering, to protect your fingers.

YOU WILL NEED

ruler

pen

4 x 4 inches of brass sheet

protective gloves

tin snips

hammer

needle file

center punch

hand drill and ¹⁄₃₂-inch drill bit

110 inches of 14-gauge brass wire

two pairs of flat-nosed pliers

round-nosed pliers

wire snips

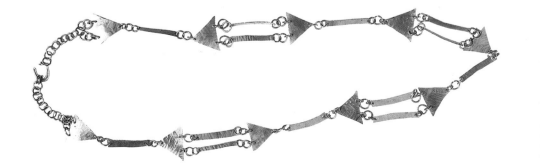

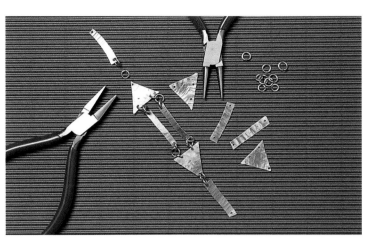

3 File the edges of the metal shapes. With a center punch, mark drill positions, three holes on the triangles and two holes on the rectangles. With a hand drill, make the necessary holes.

4 Using the brass wire and a pair of round-nosed pliers, make 109 jump rings. With two pairs of flat-nosed pliers, slightly open the jump rings and, one by one, slip them through the holes drilled in the metal shapes and then close the jump rings. Lay out the metal shapes in the sequence shown and attach the components, making sure there are three jump rings between each metal shape.

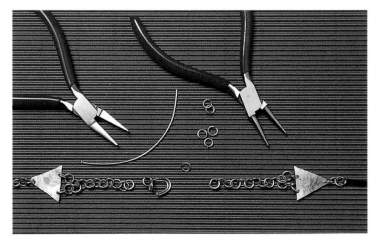

5 To finish the ends of the necklace, make a chain by linking together 14 jump rings using two pairs of flat-nosed pliers, then attach a brass coiled hook and loop fastener (see page 22).

Cupid Earrings

Here fun cake decorations are made into humorous earrings. Designs such as ballet dancers, fairies, or golden slippers can be used with corresponding saw-pierced shapes.

1 Remove the stem at the back of the decoration with a piercing saw.

2 Draw two small hearts onto the aluminum sheet. Ensure that these are in scale with the Cupids and are not too large.

3 Cut out the two hearts with the piercing saw.

4 Use resin-based glue to glue the hearts to the Cupids. Allow to set.

YOU WILL NEED

two plastic Cupid cake decorations

piercing saw frame and 2/0 saw blades

1 x 1-inch aluminum sheet

resin-based glue

center punch

drill

small ⅟₃₂-inch drill bit

emery paper

red and gray enamel paint

two jump rings

round-nosed pliers

two earring hooks

5 Mark with a center punch and drill a small hole through the top of each Cupid.

6 Remove some of the silver coating from the surface of the Cupid with emery paper.

7 Paint the clean surface with gray enamel paint and the heart with red. Allow to dry.

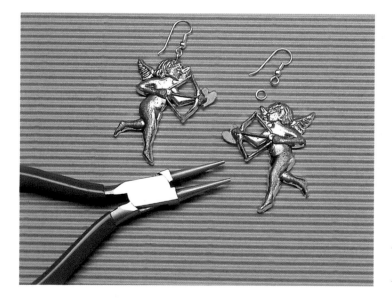

8 Attach a jump ring with round-nosed pliers and an earring hook to each earring.

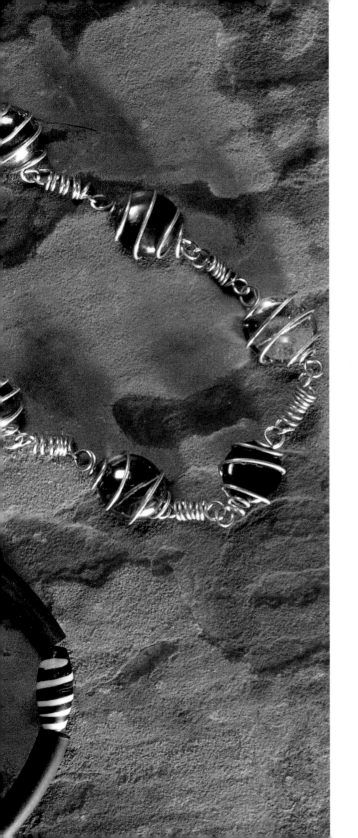

beads
shells, and stones

Shells and Pearls

Seashore finds can be transformed into exotic creations. A lot of shells are quite strong and will prove durable as earrings.

YOU WILL NEED

ten medium-sized shells

drill

small ⅟₃₂-inch drill bit

clear varnish

paintbrush

8 inches of 7-gauge copper wire

wire cutters

round-nosed pliers

six imitation pearl beads

two earring hooks

1 Select similar shells to incorporate into your earrings. Drill a small hole through each shell. To prevent splitting, drill through the central part of the shell.

2 Paint the shells with a clear varnish in a well-ventilated area. This gives them a sheen and a better appearance. Allow to dry.

3 Cut two 4-inch lengths of wire. Form a small spiral on one end of each wire. Thread on a shell, an imitation pearl, two shells, and another pearl. Repeat the process, then form a spiral.

4 Fit an earring hook to a spiral on each earring to complete.

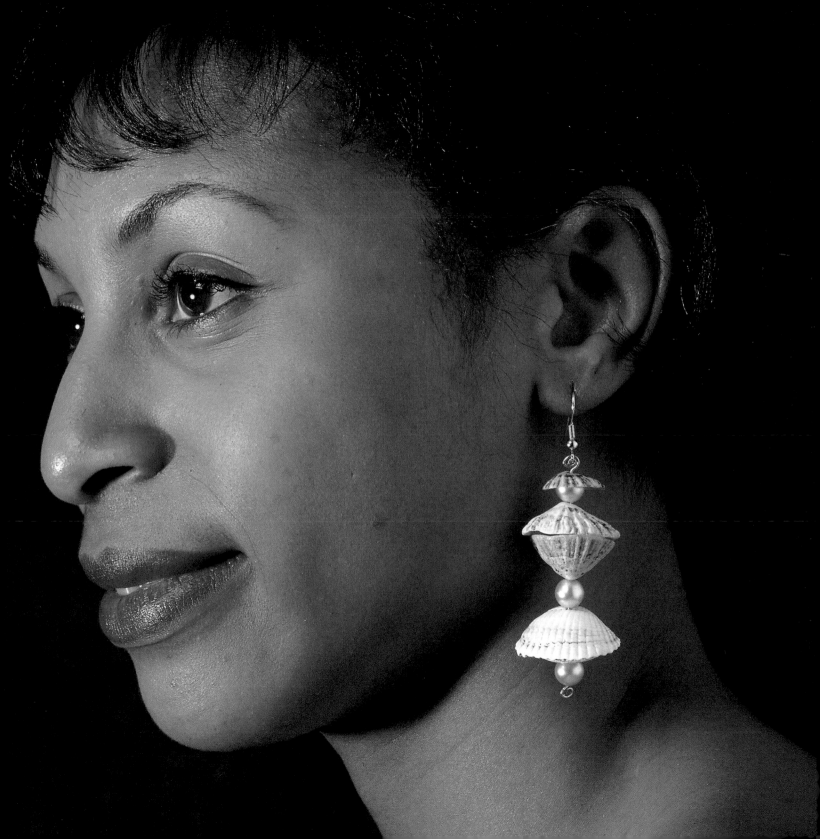

Rubber and Beads

Extruded rubber tube is used in striking contrast with large, bright beads
to create a highly tactile and modern necklace.

YOU WILL NEED

craft knife

24 inches of 11-gauge black
rubber tube

30 inches of black leather thong

scissors

fourteen varied glass beads

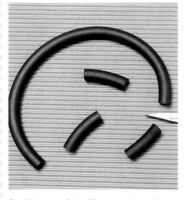

1 With a craft knife, cut the rubber
tube into 13 sections measuring
1½ inches in length.

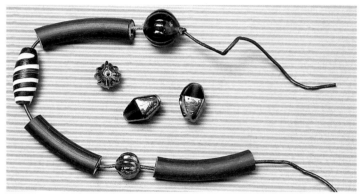

2 Tie a knot in one end of the thong. Thread the rubber tubes
and beads onto the leather thong in the order shown.

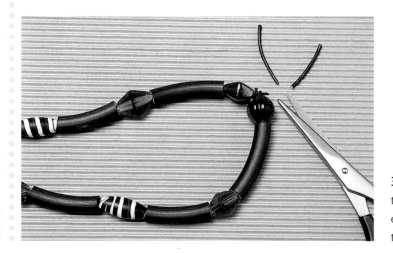

3 When all of the components are
threaded, tie a knot in the other
end of the leather thong and trim
the ends using scissors.

Natural Ceramic Beads

Earthy-colored ceramic beads are widely spaced on a linen thread to create a simple, natural effect.

scissors

2½ yards of thick linen thread

ruler

twelve natural ceramic beads

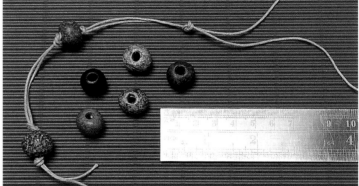

1 With the scissors, cut two lengths of linen thread measuring 45 inches each. Tie one end of each length together in a knot, approximately 2½ inches from the end of each piece of thread.

2 Slide a ceramic bead onto the threads until it rests on the knot. Tie another knot on the other side of the ceramic bead, securing it in place. Measure 2 inches from the

bead, and tie another knot. Slide on another bead and secure this with a knot. Repeat this process until all the beads are used.

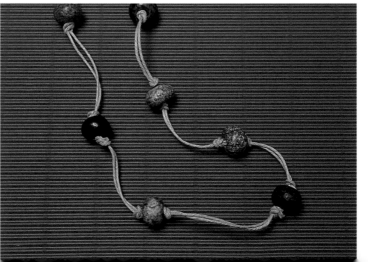

3 To finish the necklace, tie the ends of the threads together next to a bead so that the fastening is discreetly covered.

Seashell Choker

Found natural forms provide inspiration for this necklace, combining small seashells, beads, and braided linen thread.

YOU WILL NEED

2½ yards of thick linen thread

scissors

glue

needle and thread

sixteen small mixed seashell beads

five small glass beads

16 inches of black leather thong

1 Cut the natural linen thread into six 15-inch lengths. Separate the linen threads into two piles of three thread lengths.

2 Glue the ends of the three threads together and leave the glue to dry. Braid each pile of three threads and glue to secure at the other end. Leave to dry.

3 With a needle and thread, sew the two braided lengths together at one end, then sew on the shells and beads in a random fashion.

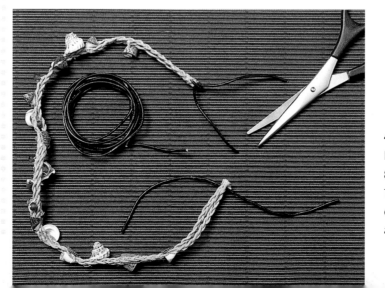

4 Sew the other ends of the braided lengths together. Cut two 8-inch lengths of leather thong. Thread the thong through the end of the two braided lengths and tie a knot to secure.

Chunky Glass Bead Choker

Hundreds of brightly-colored glass beads are strung in quantities, and combined to produce a chunky necklace design.

1 With the wire snips, cut 54 pieces of wire about 2½ inches long. (The length of the cut wires may vary depending on the size of the beads used).

2 Secure one end of the wire with the round-nosed pliers and carefully bend the wire to create a loop at the end.

3 Thread three assorted beads onto the wire.

YOU WILL NEED

wire snips

4½ yards of 14-gauge copper wire

round-nosed pliers

162 glass beads in an assortment of colors, shapes, and sizes

20 inches of black leather thong

twenty-nine glass beads which are all the same type (spacer beads)

flat-nosed pliers

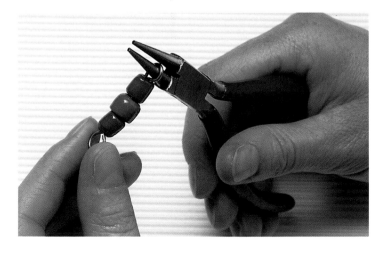

4 With the round-nosed pliers, make another loop in the other end of the wire to secure the beads.

5 Repeat steps 3 and 4 to make the other 53 beaded wires.

6 Thread the leather thong through one of the loops in the beaded wire. Interspace each series of beaded wires with a spacer bead threaded directly onto the thong. Repeat the threading and spacer beads until all of the beaded wires have been used.

7 When all the component wires have been used, thread 12 spacer beads onto the thong at each end of the mass of beaded wires. Attach a coiled hook and loop attachment (see page 22) to the ends of the leather thong, then tie a knot in the ends of the thong so that the fastening is secure.

Pebble Bracelet

It is important that the wire is wrapped around the stones tightly and securely to keep the bracelet together.

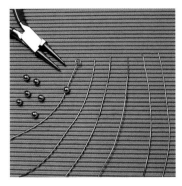

YOU WILL NEED

pebbles in various sizes

wire cutters

92 inches of metal wire

round-nosed pliers

two metal beads for each stone

flat-nosed pliers

large and small jump rings

two fasteners

varnish

1 The quantity of pebbles used will vary. The sample shown uses six, but your bangle may use more or less. Cut a length of wire approximately 4 inches long. Spiral the end using your round-nosed pliers and add a small metal bead.

2 Wrap the wire tightly around the pebble, making a small loop on either side when you reach the mid point.

3 Continue securing the pebble within the wire, then twist the two small loops (from Step 2) with your round-nosed pliers.

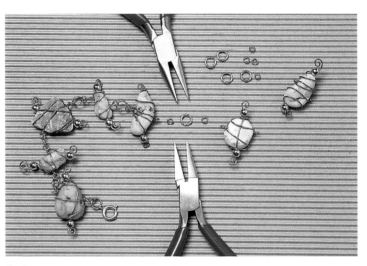

5 Place a metal bead onto the wire before making a small spiral in the wire. If you have excess wire, trim it with your wire cutters.

6 Link a small jump ring to the "twisted loop" on either side of the pebble, then pass a larger jump ring through these to link the pebbles together. Add a fastener to the ends of the bracelet.

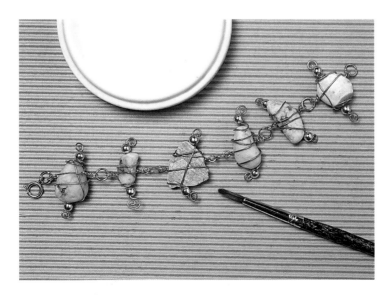

7 Varnish the bracelet all over in a well-ventilated area and leave overnight to dry.

Glass Beads and Coiled Brass

Lengths of brass wire are tightly coiled and threaded together in quantity, then interspersed with aluminum and richly-colored large glass beads to create this sophisticated, textural piece.

YOU WILL NEED

wire snips

13½ yards of 14-gauge brass wire

round-nosed pliers

eleven large, colored glass beads

40 inches of black leather thong

five aluminum beads

scissors

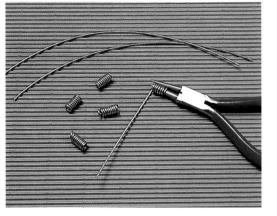

1 With wire snips, cut 64 7½-inch lengths of brass wire. Using the round-nosed pliers, coil the lengths of wire to make 64 coiled "beads."

2 Thread the glass beads, aluminum beads, and coiled wire beads onto the leather thong in the sequence shown, spacing four coiled beads between each glass or aluminum bead.

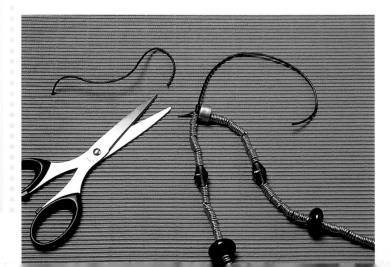

3 To finish, tie the ends of the leather thong together and then trim the ends with a pair of scissors.

Foiled Bead Choker

Brightly colored foiled glass beads are strung vertically onto a thick, flexible wire choker that is worn close to the neck.

YOU WILL NEED

6 yards of 14-gauge steel wire

round-nosed pliers

wire snips

two pairs of flat-nosed pliers

150 small foiled glass beads

clear varnish

paintbrush

1 Make 132 steel jump rings. Cut 6-inch lengths of wire, secure one end of each length in a pair of round-nosed pliers, and slowly bend the wire around one side of the pliers.

2 Continue to coil the wire around the pliers until all of the wire is used and a regular coil of wire is formed along the pliers. Make sure that the coils are evenly tightened and spaced apart.

3 Remove the coil from the pliers and, using a pair of wire snips, cut up one side of the coil.

4 To open the jump rings, use two pairs of flat-nosed pliers. Thread on another jump ring or beaded wire and close up the first jump ring to secure.

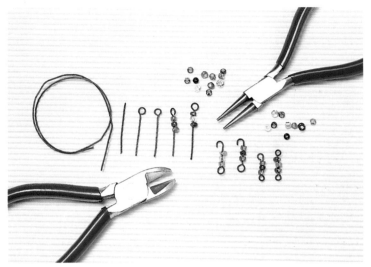

5 With the wire snips, cut 50 1-inch lengths of steel wire. With the round-nosed pliers, make a loop at one end of the wire. Thread three beads onto the wire and make a loop at the other end of the wire to secure the beads and for fastening. Repeat with the other 49 wires.

6 Link each beaded wire together using a jump ring. Once the jump ring has been threaded on, make sure it is securely closed using the flat-nosed pliers. Repeat until all of the beaded wires are linked together with jump rings as shown.

7 To complete the necklace, make a chain by linking 16 jump rings, using the flat-nosed pliers to open and close the links.

8 The chain joins onto either end of the last beaded wires, and these two chains then come together to become a single longer chain. Then, attach a coiled loop and a hook fastener (see page 22) to the last links on the choker. To finish, protect the steel wire with a layer of clear varnish applied in a well-ventilated area.

Wire and Marbles

Iridescent marbles, wrapped in wire casings, are linked together with loosely coiled sections of wire in this bold necklace.

YOU WILL NEED

wire snips

6 yards of 14-gauge galvanized steel wire

round-nosed pliers

fourteen flat-backed glass marbles

wire

1 With wire snips, cut a length of galvanized steel wire 10 inches long. Using the round-nosed pliers, make a loop in the wire and then carefully wrap the wire around the marble.

2 When the marble is wrapped in wire, make another loop in the end of the wire. These loops connect one section to another. Repeat until all of the marbles have been wrapped.

3 To make the connecting spirals. Cut a 5-inch length of wire and loosely wrap it around one side of a pair of round-nosed pliers. Bend the top and bottom loops in half.

4 Link a spiral between every marble section. Join all of the marbles and spirals together securely until they form a necklace.

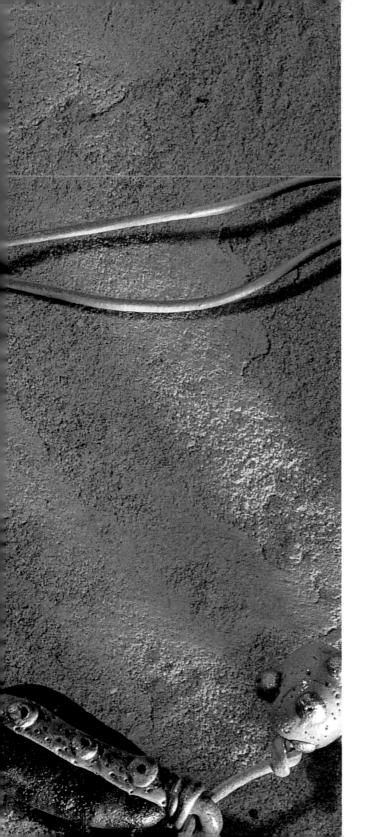

mixed media

Fantastic Plastic

"Friendly Plastic" is a new moldable plastic. When heated, it becomes soft and allows you to shape it or join pieces together. Heat the plastic in an oven at low heat instead of in hot water if you prefer. Use modeling plastic if "Friendly Plastic" is not available.

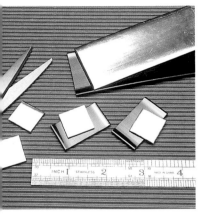

1 Cut two ¾-inch wide strips of purple plastic. Cut four ¾-inch squares of silver plastic.

2 Place a purple piece and a silver square in hot water for a few seconds until the plastic becomes soft and malleable. Carefully remove the pieces from the water using tweezers, then put the silver square on top of the purple piece. Next, press them onto a shell where the plastic will mold to the texture of the shell. You can remove the plastic right away, and it will become quite hard again after about five minutes. Repeat the process with the other purple and silver pieces.

YOU WILL NEED

ruler

scissors

one strip each of "friendly plastic" or modeling plastic in purple and silver

hot water

tweezers

seashells

drill and small drill bit or darning needle

six jump rings

round-nosed pliers

resin-based glue

two earring stems and backs

3 Heat the two remaining silver squares in water and press into a different shell surface, following Step 2.

4 Drill ⅟₃₆-inch holes or push a darning needle through the top of one side of each purple piece near the center.

5 Use the jump rings, interlocking and sealing them with the round-nosed pliers, to link the two different pieces together.

6 To complete the earrings, attach the earring stems to the back of the smaller squares with resin-based glue.

Springy Hearts and Beads

Springy hearts and beads are great fun to wear whatever the season. To change the theme you could use recycled paper, or even brightly-colored tissue paper.

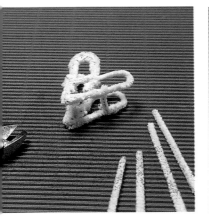

1 Make a three-dimensional heart shape frame from several pipe cleaners.

2 Cover it with strips of colored paper, securing the ends with strong adhesive.

3 Draw a heart shape the same size as the shape in Step 1 onto your piece of metal, then cut it out, using your metal shears. Glue the metal heart onto the paper-covered heart.

4 Rub the emery paper on the top of the heart, to help get an even satin finish to the metal.

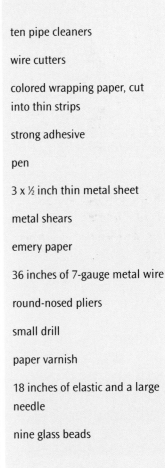

YOU WILL NEED

ten pipe cleaners

wire cutters

colored wrapping paper, cut into thin strips

strong adhesive

pen

3 x ½ inch thin metal sheet

metal shears

emery paper

36 inches of 7-gauge metal wire

round-nosed pliers

small drill

paper varnish

18 inches of elastic and a large needle

nine glass beads

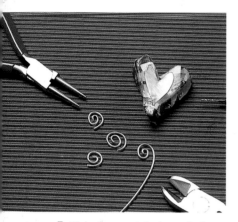

5 Make four metal wire curls, from about an inch of wire each, and glue these evenly to the sides of the heart. Drill one hole through the bottom and one through the top of the heart, through the centers of the spirals and the paper bodies.

6 Repeat Steps 1–5 until you have three complete hearts. Varnish the hearts in a well-ventilated area and leave overnight to dry.

7 With your round-nosed pliers, make a lot of little wire spirals. These will be threaded onto the elastic between the glass beads.

8 Tie a knot in the end of the elastic and thread it through the holes made in the bottoms of the hearts, the metal spirals, and the beads as shown. Tie the ends of the elastic together and glue the knot securely. Repeat the elastic threading with the holes in the tops of the hearts.

Diamante Star Medal

Soft moldable material is used to make simple settings for faux diamonds.
Use oven-bake clay for a firm fitting

1 Cut a star shape out of cardstock. Roll out the clay to a thickness of approximately ¼ inch. Lay the star template on top and lightly outline it with the scalpel.

2 Cut out the star, allowing a small ball of extra clay at all points of the star (approximately ¼ inch in diameter). Mold the clay to create a smooth shape.

YOU WILL NEED

cardstock

scissors

blue modeling clay

rolling pin

scalpel

1 inch of 14-gauge silver wire

six ¼-inch glass diamonds

twelve ⅛-inch glass diamonds

six ¹⁄₁₆-inch glass diamonds

oven

needle and thread

20 inches of 1-inch silver ribbon

pin back

resin-based glue

3 Push some wire through the side of one point of the star to make a hole. Push the glass diamonds into the center of the star and onto its points to form the desired pattern, then remove the glass diamonds, leaving the indentations in the clay. Follow manufacturer's directions to bake the star in the oven to harden it.

4 The clay will now be hardened. Stick the glass diamonds back into the star using the resin-based glue and allow them to set.

5 Using the silver wire, make a loop through the previously appointed hole in one point of your star. Thread the silver ribbon through this loop and make a bow. Cut off any excess.

6 Sew a pin back to the back of the bow.

Fossil Form

Seashells are used to make a mold to produce a fossilized-looking treasure from the sea.

1 Roll out the clay with your hands into a ½-inch thick slab. Push the wooden block evenly into the clay to make an impression approximately ¼ inch deep.

2 Use the seashells to make further impressions in the clay within the boundaries of the first impression. Remove the shells, leaving behind their forms and textures.

3 Mix the plaster of paris according to instructions and pour it carefully into the mold. Clean away any plaster from the edges.

YOU WILL NEED

self-hardening clay

2 x ¾-inch wood block

assorted small seashells

plaster of paris

2 inches of wire

scalpel

paintbrushes

blue, green and gold inks

3 inches of embroidery thread

silver-plated fish bead

⅛-inch blue glass bead

pin back

resin-based glue

4 When the plaster has begun to set, push a wire through the thin end of the plaster shape. Move it around slightly to enlarge the hole.

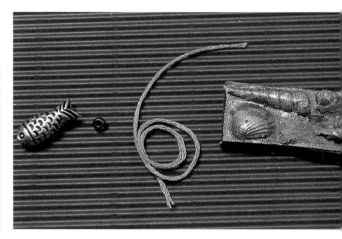

5 When the plaster has set hard, remove it from the clay and leave it to dry completely (until the plaster has become very white; overnight is a good idea).

6 Paint the plaster form using a mixture of green and blue inks. When these have dried, paint on some gold highlights.

7 Thread the embroidery thread through the hole in the brooch and then thread on the fish and blue glass beads.

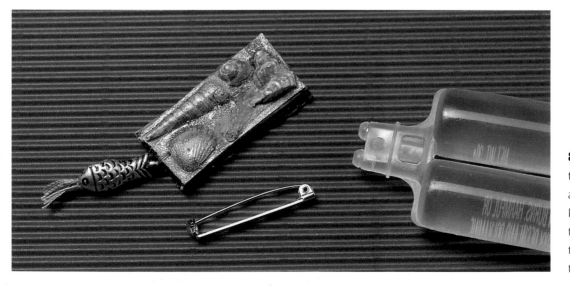

8 Knot the thread to secure it through the brooch. Cut the thread approximately ⅜ inch below the knot and open the threads to give a tassel effect. Attach the pin back to the back of the plaster form using the resin-based glue. Allow to set.

Bead and Leather Bracelet

You can change the "earthy" mood shown here by using colorful glass beads or painted ceramic beads from around the world.

YOU WILL NEED

2½ yards leather thong

scissors

hook

two smaller contrasting ceramic beads

chunky glass or ceramic beads (quantity depends on the size)

strong adhesive

wire cutters

1 Cut one length of leather thong approximately 18 inches long, fold into two, and tie a small loop knot as shown. Use the remainder of the leather to thread through the knot before tightly securing.

2 Place the loop over the hook and start by threading a smaller bead onto the shorter pair of strands. Tie the outer strands into a bow knot around the bead, once over the top of the inner strands, once below and again above.

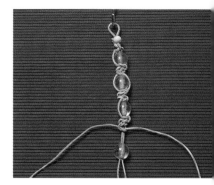

3 Repeat Step 2, but with the larger chunky beads. Stop when the bracelet is about 7 inches long.

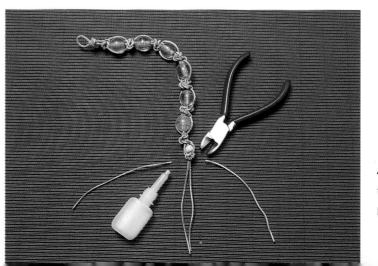

4 Add the second smaller bead, tie the outer strands, and glue into place. Cut remaining outer strands.

Silver Laced Stick Pin

Create a simple stick pin using contrasting metals laced together with fine silver wire.

YOU WILL NEED

pen

paper

glue

1 x ¾ inches of thin sheet silver

tin snips

chasing hammer

4 inches of 14-gauge brass wire

4 inches of 7-gauge silver wire

needle file

half round pliers

drill and 0.5mm drill bit

wire cutters

pin stopper

1 Draw a semi-circle on paper, the bottom edge 1 inch long, and the top of the arc ¾ inches high. Lightly glue this to the silver sheet. When dry, cut out with tin snips.

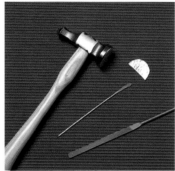

2 Remove the paper template and, using the chasing hammer, texture the surface of the silver sheet. Spread and flatten one end of the brass wire, and file the other end to a fine point.

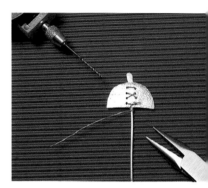

3 Lay the flattened brass wire in position across the silver shape. Drill four 0.5mm holes into the silver either side of the wire. Then, using the silver wire, lace the brass wire and silver shape together.

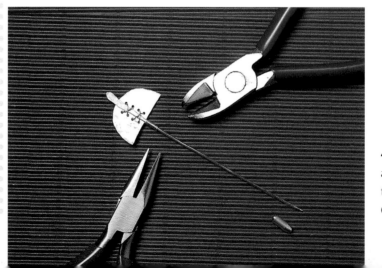

4 Spiral the loose silver wire tightly around the thicker brass pin under the silver shape for about ⅜ inch. Cut off any excess.

Leather and Fine Copper

Tightly-bound strands of leather thong are restrained with fine copper wire and joined with large copper jump rings in an unusual chain formation.

YOU WILL NEED

scissors

2½ yards of black leather thong

2 x 1½-inch cardboard

36 inches of 7-gauge copper wire

52 inches of 14-gauge copper wire

flat-nosed pliers

round-nosed pliers

wire snips

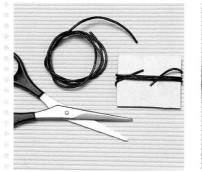

1 With scissors, cut nine equal lengths of black leather thong and wrap one around the piece of cardboard.

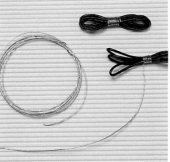

2 Cut nine lengths of fine copper wire. Slide the leather thong carefully off the piece of card and bind a length of copper wire tightly around the thong, ensuring the loose ends are tied under the wire. Repeat for the remaining pieces.

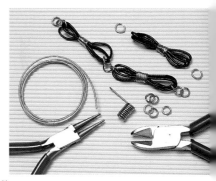

3 Make 22 jump rings out of the 14-gauge copper wire. Use three jump rings to link the bundles of leather thong together, attaching the jump rings directly around the coiled leather loops.

4 When all of the leather sections have been linked together, make and attach a coiled copper wire hook and loop fastening (see page 22).

Silk and Mother-of-Pearl

Mother-of-pearl buttons sewn onto a black silk ribbon make a simple
yet elegant choker.

YOU WILL NEED

14 inches of ¾-inch wide black
silk ribbon

scissors

1 inch of ⅝-inch Velcro

needle and black thread

five mother-of-pearl buttons

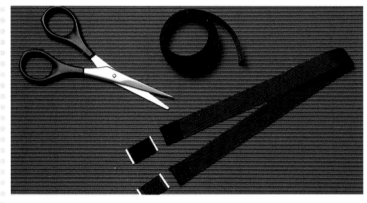

1 Measure a length of ribbon to fit loosely around the neck. With a pair
of scissors, cut the ribbon and sew the Velcro to each of the ends. Bend
the ribbon in half to find the center.

2 Using a needle and thread, sew
the first button in the center of the
silk ribbon.

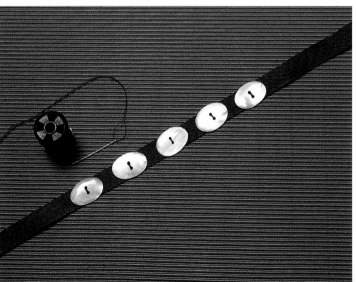

3 Continue to sew the buttons, at
even distances from one another, on
either side of the center button until
all five buttons have been used.

Perspex and Silver Stars

Simple and elegant, these star drop earrings are made from black acrylic sheet.
Other colors or clear plastic could be used with copper or brass wire and beads.

1 Make a star template from cardstock. Cover the Perspex sheet with masking tape and use the template to draw two stars.

2 Saw-pierce the two stars out of the Perspex and remove the tape.

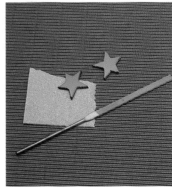

3 File and smooth the edges of the stars with emery paper and a needle file to remove all traces of cutting marks.

4 Center-punch the center of each star, then drill a hole through it.

YOU WILL NEED

cardstock

1½ x 3 inches of ⅛-inch black Perspex sheet

masking tape

piercing saw frame and 2/0 blades

emery paper

flat needle file

center punch

drill and 1/16-inch drill bit

10 inches of 14-gauge sterling silver round section wire

four small silver beads

wire cutters

chain-nosed pliers

hammer

two earring hooks

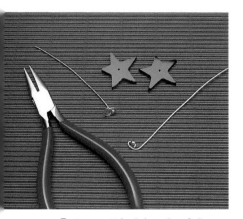

5 Cut two 5-inch lengths of silver wire. Insert a bead onto one end and curl the wire around to prevent the bead from falling off, then form a small spiral around the bead. Repeat this process with the other wire.

6 Push a wire through the hole in each Perspex star and insert another bead onto the wire. Bend the wire so that it runs flat against the back of the star shape.

7 Form a wavy pattern with the remaining wire and cut to your desired length. Make a small loop at the very end and hammer the wire flat.

8 Attach earring hooks to the top loops of wire to complete the earrings.

Suppliers

USA

The Jewelry Institute of America
40 Sims Avenue
Providence, RI 02909

Equipment and Tools Suppliers

All Craft Tool Supply Company Inc.
666 Pacific Street
Brooklyn, NY 11217

Beadbox
1290 N. Scottsdale Road, Suite 104
Tempe, Arizona 85281-1703

Beadworks
905 South Ann Street
Baltimore, MD 21231

C R Hill Co.
2734 W 11 Mile Road
Berkley, MI 48072

Fire Mountain Gems
28195 Redwood Highway
Cave Junction, OR 97523

Helby Import Co.
1501 South Park Avenue
Linden, NJ 07036
Wholesale to specialty bead shops

International Bead and Jewelry Supply
2368 Kettner Boulevard
San Diego, CA 92101

Paul H Gesswein's Co Inc.
255 Hancock Avenue
Bridgeport, CT 06605

Rings & Things
P.O. Box 450
Spokane, WA 99210-0450

Swest Inc.
10803 Composite Drive
Dallas, TX 75220

T S I Jewelry Supply
101 Nickerson Street
P.O. Box 9266
Seattle, WA 98109

Many craft retailers and chain stores like
Michaels, A.C. Moore, and Pear Art & Craft
Supply, carry jewelry making products;
check you local phone directory.

Index